THE COVER: Before the young U.S. adopted the Stars and Stripes as official flag in 1777, a popular ensign was a serpent flag like this one. Flags of this type began appearing around 1774. A picture of a snake cut into pieces to symbolize the disunited colonies, bearing the words "Join or Die," had been circulated in previous years; now the unsevered serpent was used to symbolize unity and defiance, as evoked by the slogan "Don't tread on me."

THE **LIFE** HISTORY OF THE UNITED STATES

Volume 1: Before 1775

THE NEW WORLD

THE TIME-LIFE LIBRARY OF BOATING

HUMAN BEHAVIOR

THE ART OF SEWING

THE OLD WEST

THE EMERGENCE OF MAN

THE AMERICAN WILDERNESS

THE TIME-LIFE ENCYCLOPEDIA OF GARDENING

LIFE LIBRARY OF PHOTOGRAPHY

THIS FABULOUS CENTURY

FOODS OF THE WORLD

TIME-LIFE LIBRARY OF AMERICA

TIME-LIFE LIBRARY OF ART

GREAT AGES OF MAN

LIFE SCIENCE LIBRARY

THE LIFE HISTORY OF THE UNITED STATES

TIME READING PROGRAM

LIFE NATURE LIBRARY

LIFE WORLD LIBRARY

FAMILY LIBRARY:

    HOW THINGS WORK IN YOUR HOME

    THE TIME-LIFE BOOK OF THE FAMILY CAR

    THE TIME-LIFE FAMILY LEGAL GUIDE

    THE TIME-LIFE BOOK OF FAMILY FINANCE

THE LIFE HISTORY OF THE UNITED STATES

Consulting Editor, Henry F. Graff

Volume 1: Before 1775

THE NEW WORLD

by Richard B. Morris

and the Editors of

TIME-LIFE BOOKS

TIME-LIFE BOOKS, NEW YORK

THE AUTHOR, Richard B. Morris, is an outstanding authority on America's colonial period. A native of New York, Dr. Morris is Gouverneur Morris Professor Emeritus of History at Columbia University and has been a visiting professor at various universities from Hawaii to Paris. He is editor of the *Encyclopedia of American History* and of the authorized compilation of the John Jay papers, and co-editor of the *New American Nation* series. He has written many volumes on American history, including *The American Revolution Reconsidered* and *The Peacemakers*, which won the Bancroft Prize in 1966.

THE CONSULTING EDITOR for this series, Henry F. Graff, is Professor of History at Columbia University in New York.

Valuable assistance in preparing this volume was given by Roger Butterfield, who served as picture consultant to the Editor; photographers Eliot Elisofon and George Silk; Editorial Production, Norman Airey; Library, Benjamin Lightman; Picture Collection, Doris O'Neil; Photographic Laboratory, George Karas; TIME-LIFE News Service, Murray J. Gart; Revisions Staff, Harold C. Field, Joan Chambers.

CONTENTS

A heroic segment of time

ALL men find comfort and reassurance in knowing how their civilization developed and where in the grand arrangement of events it stands at the moment. But we Americans at this juncture in the 20th Century have a particular need to take our historical bearings. Prodigious changes have set their seal upon our generation. The convulsions of two World Wars cracked and finally shattered the wall of isolation behind which our countrymen had taken shelter for so long. For the first time since the 18th Century, we are again face-to-face with the rest of the world. We see now what was for so long hidden from view: we are permanently "entangled" with the family of man. Acknowledging this to ourselves once more—a process paradoxically difficult for a nation of immigrants—has given us a chance to place our history in a fresh perspective.

America's position among nations has been special from the very beginning. Separated from Europe by 3,000 miles of ocean, our shores were at first merely a westward projection of the European powers—a plaything of kings and queens. But legions of ordinary people, most of them forever nameless in the pages of history, swarmed across the Atlantic and—out of disparate elements—molded on this continent a luxuriant and unique culture.

To be sure, the men and women who came from the other side of the ocean were not consciously the harbingers of a better life for mankind. But they were forced by the demands of a strange and awesome setting to become experimenters, constantly reworking the old and the familiar into New World styles. Their failures were often gargantuan and their successes sometimes only fitfully held, but from the start they seemed to make progress: tomorrow would be not only different from today, it would be better.

Because American history seems to fall naturally into six eras, it is so divided in this work. The culmination of the first era, which begins in the mists of prehistory, was the achievement of national independence and the writing of the Constitution, a twin climax, as we see it now, to 180 years of preparation. These events are recounted in Volumes 1 and 2.

The decades comprising the second period—treated in Volumes 3 and 4—tested keenly the political and social institutions we had brought into being, for they now served a country which dwarfed in grandeur even the fondest dreams of the Founding Fathers. The conquest of the American West, furthermore, presented a resplendent proving ground for the nation's mettle, intellectual as well as physical.

Like all high drama, however, ours contained a tragic element, and the entire world watched to see the outcome. By the middle of the 19th Century the incubus of slavery had fastened itself tightly on the country, and signs were unmistakable that it would not vanish on its own—that it would have to be torn out root and branch. The Civil War—the core of the third major period, which is treated in Volumes 5 and 6—may

have been Armageddon or it may have been only evidence of a momentary failure in our political system. But not to be questioned is the fact that the Civil War was the sundering sword of flame in our story. We went into the war primarily an agricultural people; we came out of it not yet an urban and industrial society but inexorably moving in that direction.

After the Civil War, in the last decades of the 19th Century, our adaptation to the remarkable environment we created out of abundant natural resources transformed the whole of American society. This fourth era in our history is the subject of Volumes 7 and 8. The accommodation that came to pass was more far-reaching than anything the 17th Century settlers had made. Americans seemed animated now by boundless new energy: they had become a nation of builders and doers, drawing from every reach of the earth vigorous and aggressive people of like mind and purpose to join them in their work.

At the turn of the century, strengthened by numbers and emboldened by military power, we Americans ventured, at first uncertainly, back into the world. This, our fifth era, extended into the 1930s. As related in Volumes 9 and 10, it was in this period that we undertook the thankless business of developing an overseas empire; for the moment, millions of Americans were transfixed by its possibilities. If in the long run the experiment in imperialism failed, it nevertheless helped to prepare us for some of the complexities that have made living in the 20th Century at once so grimly dangerous and so fascinating.

In our own day, which constitutes the sixth era, we have not lacked momentous events to put our judgment and ingenuity to the proof. An account of these episodes, presented in Volumes 11 and 12, completes the story as we have seen it—a heroic segment of the turbulent river of time.

The six historians who have written the narrative text for THE LIFE HISTORY OF THE UNITED STATES deal with the periods in which they are expert. The treatment of each period differs from that of the others in tone and style, as befits the range and diversity of the material under scrutiny and the independent viewpoints which the writers have brought to their work. The result is a series of broad, personalized interpretations entirely appropriate to the subject.

Men will argue everlastingly about what constitutes "true" history. But they know what "good" history is. It is a vivid painting, never a neutral photograph, of what has gone before. It is done in many colors and strokes, and on a huge canvas. It lauds and blames; it describes, it analyzes, it causes pain; it excites and it ennobles. It revels in the beautiful and the moral; it deplores the mean and the shameful. It neither trumpets shrilly over the victories, nor tarries indecently on the blemishes. In brief, good history reveals the past, as these volumes do, in a bright and penetrating light. And, out of a thoughtful appreciation of that portion of mankind's story which we have already witnessed, it inspires in us a fresh confidence to face whatever secrets and surprises the future hides.

—HENRY F. GRAFF
Professor of History
Columbia University

1. AMERICA BEFORE COLUMBUS

MAN reached the New World at least 30,000 or 40,000 years ago and perhaps even 100,000 years ago. As geologic time is counted, this is only yesterday, but it represents a far longer stretch of continuous occupation than scientists had imagined until recently. Of these very first Americans there are only a few tantalizing traces. But their successors left behind imposing ruins, enduring monuments to advanced societies that existed in North America centuries before Columbus landed on its shores. There was culture here, religion and prosperity—in some respects there was even more sophistication than existed in Europe during the same period. Huge pyramids that are now overgrown with vegetation in the Midwest mark the sites of long-forgotten religious rituals. Apartment-house communities built into precipitous cliffs in the Southwest testify to primitive architectural skill and social harmony. Satellite towns whose roads lead to a central six-and-a-half-square-mile city in southern Illinois reflect political acumen.

Unfortunately, none of these early Americans developed a written language. This lack has hampered the investigations of scholars, who remain curious about the pre-Columbian Indians' intellectual pursuits, laws and everyday lives. Even their spoken tongues were so varied that some tribes, separated only by a few miles, had to use sign language to talk with one another. As a consequence, what is known of the first Americans has the quality of a tortured reconstruction flawed by disconcerting gaps.

THE NATIVE AMERICAN, a resident of the continent for at least 200 centuries when the white man arrived, is shown in the person of a proud, fierce chief of the Blackfoot tribe.

There is considerable evidence to support the widely held theory that migrants from Asia first reached North America during an ice age. They presumably entered during those periods when the sea level was lowered as water froze into advancing ice sheets creating a wide land bridge between Siberia and Alaska. Harried by cold, searching for more abundant game, men could —and probably did—cross this causeway from Asia into the Western Hemisphere. There are definite signs of such a geologic change, written for all time in the rock strata of the earth's crust.

Until recent years the dating of the migration had been a far more difficult problem. The signs of human handiwork that paleontologists, geologists, archeologists and anthropologists at scattered points had happened upon or had dug up demonstrate that man had been living in the New World for thousands of years. But since World War II, radiocarbon 14 dating, a by-product of atomic research, has made it possible to achieve much surer agreement than ever before among the scientists. Carbon 14, a radioactive isotope present in living organisms in fixed proportions, disintegrates after death at a known rate. Thus measurements of the residue in charred bones or charcoal deposits can serve as a fairly accurate atomic calendar.

The testimony of this and other dating techniques raises the possibility of extremely ancient human settlements—one tentative measurement places the time at 100,000 years ago. More certain dating techniques indicate that man certainly lived in America by 25,000 B.C., at the time when Europe's Cro-Magnon man was daubing hunting scenes on cave walls in the Dordogne region of France. There was apparently a relatively speedy dispersal of Asiatic settlers throughout the Americas, from the Bering Strait to Tierra del Fuego. No one any longer doubts that the main line of early settlement ran from northeastern Asia into Alaska and then southward as far as the Strait of Magellan. Yet circumstantial evidence points to the possibility of another, much more recent movement over the ocean from the west, this time by Polynesian seafarers from the isles of the South Pacific, possibly the Marquesas. These intrepid voyagers may have reached the Pacific coast of South America; in any case, about 500 years ago they most certainly did reach Easter Island where they left mementos in the form of statues and myths.

Even before the Polynesians pointed their long outrigger canoes toward the South American shore, another breed of venturers, the Norsemen, had triumphed over a hostile ocean and made a landfall on the northeastern coast of North America. Their coming ranks as a historical oddity. It happened yet yielded no enduring results, exerted no influence and for centuries was all but

The Indian calumet, or peace pipe, sometimes lacked a bowl. In that case smoke was sucked from tobacco burning in a dish. Pipes, about two and a half feet long, were decorated with eagles' quills or occasionally with women's hair. They were used not only at peace talks but at all important discussions.

forgotten. Yet such was the daring of the Norsemen that their story still seizes the imagination of all who read it. Two old sagas tell that story. The more reliable account tells of a Greenlander, Leif (the Lucky) Ericsson, who sailed from Norway in the summer of the year 1000 to carry the Christian faith to his pagan homeland. "For a long time he was tossed about upon the ocean," but at last reached an unknown shore. It was the New World. Leif named his discovery Vinland, probably after wild grapes he saw growing there. Most scholars believe that Vinland was somewhere on the New England coast; however, this exploration was not an isolated one. Evidence exists of a landing farther north, in Newfoundland, that was the beginning of a settlement, a sizable community that may have lasted as long as 50 years. Its end seems to have been caused by violent contact with a strange and hostile people, the "Skrellings," or as they were much later to be called, Eskimos. Apparently knowledge of these explorations never went beyond Scandinavia, and nearly 500 years were to pass before another European ventured toward the Vinland shore.

Grotesque wooden masks similar to this one were worn by Iroquois medicine men to scare away evil spirits of the forest. The mask was carved directly into a tree trunk to imbue the effigy with the tree's living spirit. Then the mask was separated from the tree, decorated and trimmed with human hair.

IN the long history of the New World, the Norse incursion was an isolated incident. Indian development went on as before. That development, though uneven, achieved remarkable results. Its unevenness is understandable, since the original settlers probably migrated in separate waves over a long period of time and they varied considerably in their physical characteristics. They also differed extraordinarily in their skills as craftsmen and warriors, and in their talents for political organization.

The first arrivals from Asia brought with them a primitive Stone Age culture and a knowledge of how to use fire. In time some of them learned how to work metal. Others never advanced beyond stone weapons and tools. New skills like basket weaving, new weapons like the bow and arrow, new domesticated plants like corn appeared. But these developments were only a token of the fantastic splendors that were to follow. In the jungles of Central America, the Valley of Mexico and the Peruvian highlands, flowered great civilizations comparable to those of the Mediterranean and of Western Europe. The Maya, the Aztec and the Inca empires rank as high-water marks in the story of human achievement.

If such peaks of true civilization were not reached north of the Rio Grande, they were more closely approached than anyone has been willing to admit until recently. The vast territory that was to become the United States and Canada was not always empty land, untilled and untraveled except by a few bands of rude savages. In two separate areas about 1,000 years ago, agricultural societies, apparently derived from Central American origins, developed considerable sophistication, and one became a complex, rich culture dominating much of the continent.

Stylized images of sacred buffalo figures are portrayed in this copy of a Navaho sand painting. The border running around three sides represents a mirage. This ritual design was executed by a medicine man for an ailing patient. Such designs are still made by pouring dry pigments on a sand base.

All over the arid Southwest after about 1000 A.D., farming based on irrigation, some ingenious and elaborate, arose. The principal crops were corn, squash and beans, abundant enough to sustain a settled population with a talent for beautifully designed baskets and pottery. Some of these people lived in apartment-house towns, later called pueblos, clusters of as many as 800 rooms built on top of one another. The most remarkable of these complexes were built in the high plateaus of New Mexico and Arizona, where, apparently for reasons of defense, the adobe houses were tucked into ledges in the faces of vertical cliffs. The residents—men, children, even women with babies on their backs

—climbed up toeholds in the cliffs every day to work in the fields above.

The pueblo towns of the Southwest, though notable achievements, were outshone in the Midwest, near St. Louis, by an Indian city that is now called Cahokia after a group of Indians who, much later, lived nearby. (The original name is unknown.) At the height of its prosperity, in about 1150 A.D., it was a true metropolis, with a population of about 30,000 living inside the city limits and another 10,000 in the metropolitan area stretching perhaps 15 miles around, in some of the most fertile cropland in the world. The central city was an imposing assemblage of civil and religious buildings, including one temple, a pyramid 10 stories tall. Outside wooden walls was an unusual structure, a "sun-circle" that seems to have served as a crude, Stonehenge-like astronomical observatory. This thriving community was the headquarters of a commercial city-state. It produced salt from well-organized refineries and had factories making hoes from flint and ceremonial pipes from soft stone. These and other goods were traded for minerals and furs as far as the Dakotas to the west, the Gulf Coast to the south and the Appalachians to the east. Traders even carried a wide variety of goods from Cahokia by boat over the waterways of the Mississippi River and Great Lakes systems.

By the time Europeans arrived, the glory that was Cahokia had vanished. The city was a ruin, marked only by the forest-covered remains of the mounds

WIDE AND VARIED WORLD
OF THE INDIANS

This map shows where some of the 500-odd tribal societies of American Indians probably lived at the time of Columbus. They were scattered across the continent in forests, on the plains, in the deserts. They were often on the move: the Omaha from the Ohio basin into the plains, the Chippewa spreading over the Great Lakes area. In years to come some Indian nations would disappear. But the names of the great tribes still endure approximately where the map puts them—on mountains (Mt. Shasta), on rivers (Penobscot), on cities (Natchez) and on states (Alabama).

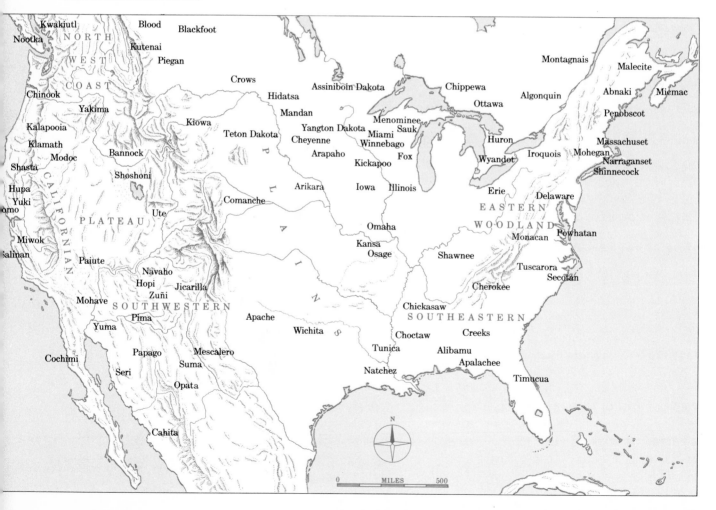

that had been prominent features of the metropolis. (Other tribes of the Midwest and South also built similar mounds, and all these peoples are often referred to as the Moundbuilders.)

Early explorers puzzled over the remnants of Cahokia, but failed to grasp their significance. By the 15th Century what is now the United States and Canada was largely wilderness populated by no more than a million Indians, compared with perhaps 15 million in Central and South America. Diversity was the hallmark of the North American Indian tribes. In temperament they ranged from the peaceful Pima of Arizona to the belligerent Iroquois of New York. Some were town dwellers like the Pueblo, others nomadic hunters like the Apache. Some, like the Kwakiutl of the Pacific Northwest, had a competitive, almost capitalistic society, and some, like a number of the eastern tribes, were more communally oriented. Even when they lived close to each other, as in the case of the Hopi and Navaho, they did not necessarily look alike, speak alike, live alike or even pray alike. What they had in common were fatal deficiencies. They lacked horses, and their weapons and tools were primitive. But their worst liability was ineffective political organization. Most of them could not unite, which meant that an organized invader could immediately put them in peril.

There were literally hundreds of different patterns of North American Indian life (see page 16), and scholars trying to create some sort of order have proposed different systems of classification. One method has been to consider the continental domain as comprising seven cultural areas: Southwestern, Plateau, California, Northwest Coast, Plains, Eastern Woodland and Southeastern. These seven divisions are at best approximate because the regions overlapped, and within each there were frequent and sharp variations in the mode of living. Each of the seven areas nevertheless had certain salient customs and characteristics.

The arid Southwestern Area was a land remarkable for its settled farming tribes—the Pima, Papago and Pueblo farmers. In the harsh Plateau Area north of the Pueblo were the primitive Shoshoni, who lived in comparative isolation, hunted deer, and gathered wild seeds and piñon nuts. In strong contrast to the communal Pueblo life, Shoshoni organization rarely rose above the family level. Even more isolated and primitive were the tribes of the California Area. They were acorn eaters, hunters of small game, occasional fishermen and even less frequent farmers.

F ARTHER north, life grew in complexity. The Indians of the Northwest Coast Area, who ruled the region from the Columbia River up into Alaska, were a maritime people who were remarkably skilled in working the lavish stands of towering evergreens. They fished for salmon in the great rivers, plied the coast in their dugout canoes and carved their towering totem poles into fantastically detailed genealogical documents. They also constructed elaborate social structures. The Kwakiutl, for example, had a many-layered social order that descended in sharp steps from the chiefs and nobles at the top to luckless slaves—war captives or debtors—at the bottom. In economic affairs the Northwest Coast folk believed in the institution of private property to a far greater extent than almost any other Indian group. It was possible for a tribesman to acquire wives, houses, fishing stations—even names—by purchase, inheritance or force of arms.

A gaudily painted brave of the Fox tribe, a shirt knotted rakishly about his waist, is shown ready for war in this French picture of about 1730. The artist noted that the typical Fox headdress was copied by other Indians, but the tribe itself was widely disliked. Though courageous and daring, the Fox were notorious for their avaricious, quarrelsome and dishonest ways.

Separated from the rainy forests of the Northwest by the massive palisades of the Rockies, the Plains Area stretched east and southeast, an almost limitless expanse of grasslands rolling all the way from the mountains to the Mississippi. Until the horse was introduced by the Spaniards in the Southwest, the plains were quiet. Farming tribes like the Mandan and the Arikara led a settled existence along the rivers of the region and occasionally hunted buffalo. The huge herds of buffalo that wandered through the region were also followed by nomads like the Comanche and Apache, but buffalo hunting afoot yielded too small a reward either to attract or to sustain a large population. The serenity of the Great Plains would be shattered when horse-mounted tribes like the Blackfoot and the Sioux moved in to make the grasslands their great hunting range and battleground.

East of the plains the forests of the Eastern Woodland Area reached all the way from the Mississippi to the Atlantic Coast. Here were the tribes whose names and deeds were to ring through colonial history. Most widely dispersed and numerous were the tribes linked by the Algonquian group of languages: among others, the Abnaki; the Mohegan; the Narragansett; the Delaware, who formed a powerful Middle Atlantic confederacy; and the strong Powhatan confederation of Virginia. The Algonquian group ranged from Canada to Virginia and from the Atlantic to the Appalachian Mountains and occupied territory west of the mountains around the Great Lakes to the northern plains. The men stalked deer and rode the streams and lakes in their birchbark canoes, while the women tended small plots of corn, squash and beans. They lived in villages made up of domed wigwams and protected by fortifications that were made of tree trunks.

This graceful fish design on a clay dish was made 1,000 years ago by the Mimbres tribe of the American Southwest. The dish, buried in its owner's grave, had a hole drilled through its center out of which the fish's soul was expected to emerge and accompany the dead person's soul into the afterworld.

THE Algonquian Indians needed these wooden walls and more to save them from the wrath of the Iroquois, who had gradually pushed their way north along the Appalachian chain to drive a wedge into Algonquian territory. At the time of the coming of the white man, the Iroquois still had only a precarious hold in upper New York. Here sometime in the 16th Century the legendary Hiawatha preached unity to the Iroquois and ultimately convinced them of the advantages of peaceful confederation. Whatever Hiawatha may have said or done, the five Iroquois tribes—the Seneca, Cayuga, Onondaga, Oneida and Mohawk—showed an unusual aptitude for political organization. Banding together, they built a political system superior to anything ever created by the other Indian peoples of the Northeast. The league endured for at least two centuries and, while they never fought each other, member tribes and even subgroups within tribes often disagreed with each other and pursued their own policies to the inevitable end of weakening the external power of the Iroquois confederation.

Scarcely less formidable than the Iroquois were the warlike Muskhogean tribes of the Southeastern Area—the Creek confederacy, the Chickasaw and Choctaw. The proud Creek, numbering about 30,000 people in 50 loosely knit farming communities, dominated the greater part of present-day Georgia and Alabama. To the west, in what is now Mississippi, lay the lands of their kin and foe, the Chickasaw. The bellicose Chickasaw waged war not only against the Creek but also against the related Choctaw, who farmed the river bottomlands in Alabama and Mississippi. North of these quarreling Muskhogean tribes, living in the mountains of what was later to become Georgia and the

Carolinas, were the Cherokee, a progressive agricultural tribe that spoke an Iroquoian tongue.

The glaring deficiencies in political organization might of themselves have been sufficient to ensure the tragic destruction of Indian life by the Europeans. But to this handicap of their own making there was added the critical factor of a geography advantageous to the enterprising adventurers from the Old World. Once the white man had mastered the Atlantic, the continent lay open to his grasp. The explorers who reconnoitered the highly indented and hospitable eastern coast of North America found bays, harbors, inlets and rivers that offered attractive sites for initial settlement and, later on, easy access to the interior. To explorers and settlers alike, American waters were highways rather than obstacles. It was only natural that the first English colonists should pick sheltered harbor sites in New England and settle along the great rivers of the south, like the James and the York.

The Tidewater belt of coastal land ranged in altitude from sea level to about 400 feet, and fanned out from a narrow coastal strip about 50 miles wide in New England to a region up to 200 miles wide along the southern Atlantic coast. The Tidewater country was most accessible, had generally fertile soil and enjoyed abundant rainfall. Its western limits were marked by the fall line of its rivers, where waterfalls and rapids marked the rise to the uplands of the Piedmont Plateau. The Piedmont extended all the way from northern New England to Alabama, rising to as high as 2,000 feet at the edge of its western limit, the Appalachian Mountains. This higher ground had a more fertile soil, a more temperate climate and as much rainfall as the coastal plain. After the Tidewater had become crowded and its thin soil depleted, the Piedmont would beckon the settlers deeper into the continent.

Beyond the Piedmont rose the Appalachian Highland, which would stand for a while as a barrier to the English colonists. But even that barrier had two gateways: the valleys of the Hudson and Mohawk pointing the way west, and the Hudson-Champlain passage to the north. The western route was the great Iroquois war trail, an ideal passageway, the use of which would have to await the growth of English colonial strength. The northern route led only into what was to become French territory. Southward from Pennsylvania stretched the Shenandoah Valley, a fertile ribbon of land between the eastern and western ranges of the Appalachians. It offered an indirect way west to the Cumberland Gap or the valley of the Tennessee and then out to the more open country beyond.

The French and the Spaniards were even better favored by nature for their advances into the great central basin drained by the Mississippi. In the north the St. Lawrence provided a route around one end of the Appalachian barrier; in the south the Alabama Black Belt and the entire Gulf Coast offered easy passage around the other end.

O N the eve of Columbus' arrival, the patterns of their life may have seemed to the Indians fixed and unalterable, the barriers to alteration impassable. But in time, every barrier would yield to the driving energy of the settlers. Nothing would stop the white man once he had secured a beachhead in the New World. He would climb over, swing around or thread through all geographical obstacles. He would drive the Indians into a long westerly retreat. And he would take over the American land to make it uniquely his own.

Knowledge of the exact meaning and function of this crude effigy died with the prehistoric Indians of the Cumberland River in Tennessee who carved it. Modeled in sandstone and over a foot high, the squatting figure probably had a religious purpose in honoring a great deity or revered ancestor.

Over 300 years ago, an Indian of the now-extinct Dalles tribe of the Pacific Northwest carved this two-foot-high lava owl. Fashioned with stone tools, the sculpture, apparently of a clan ancestor or a guardian spirit, has a chevron pattern to suggest feathers and was probably colored with paint.

15

In feathers and fish-bladder earrings, a 16th Century tattooed Florida chief exhorts his rapt warriors.

The Indians as white men met them

T HE American Indian, in the eyes of the white men who first met him, was a puzzle. The Indian was generous. He was cruel and he dearly loved merciless war. For efficiency in combat he kept his body strong and hard. In battle he was courageous, and if captured he endured torture by taunting his captors and singing his war songs until death silenced him. These qualities, highly esteemed by the strong, cruel and war-loving whites who came to America in the early 16th Century, helped create a long-lived mythology.

But, from the first contact, there were curious, sensitive newcomers who labored to picture the Indian as he really was. Two of the earliest were Jacques Le Moyne, a Frenchman, who in 1564 depicted Saturiwa, a Florida Timucua chief, scattering ceremonial water *(above)* to show how he wanted blood to flow in a war, and John White, an Englishman, who in 1586 painted North Carolina coastal Indians *(right)* fishing. Over 300 years, as Europeans slowly filled the old 48 states and met the incredible variety of Indian civilizations, other artists, including dedicated George Catlin, worked to capture forever their differing lives. A gallery of revealing pictures of the many facets of Indian life, before white men's ways and vices changed it, appears on the pages that follow.

SKILLED FISHERMEN, Roanoke Indians *(opposite)* trap fish in reed weirs and spear others in shallows *(back ground)*. At night, fires in canoes drew fish to the nets

The manner of their fishing.

A Cannow

Their greene corn

Corne newly sprong

Their sitting at meate

The place of solemne prayer

house wherin the Tombe of their Herounds standeth

SECOTON

A Ceremony in their praye[r]
strange iestures and songs da[
abowt posts carued on the t[

A formal way of life in simple coastal villages

Oₙ the Eastern Seaboard, from the Florida Keys north to Maine, were a host of small Indian tribes which scholars now group by language families—Muskhogean, Iroquoian, Algonquian. They lived in tiny villages, perhaps a few hundred Indians to a group, much like the North Carolina village of Secotan *(left)* painted by John White in 1586. They grew corn, tobacco, squash and other crops unknown to Europe, and the men fished and hunted deer. For war or great occasions they adorned their hair, painted their cheeks and dressed in meticulously prescribed fashions. They had stylized ways for praying to their gods and for feasting. Often they raided each other's villages, taking scalps and prisoners, but they generally let the enemy know just who had called, thus both increasing the victims' rage and inviting a return engagement. This caused deaths and grieving, and there was a proper mode *(right)* to express that, too.

A CHIEF'S WIFE with pearl necklace and tattooed arm bands *(left)* wears an elaborately fringed deerskin skirt. Her daughter, carrying a European doll, has only a necklace and girdle.

WIDOWS OF WARRIORS sorrow at the feet of a Timucua chief *(above)* of Florida in 1564. As part of their mourning, women cut their hair. When it was grown back they could remarry.

FAMILY DINNER, 16th Century North Carolina style *(below),* consists of a platter of boiled corn. The Indians were also fond of stews of deer meat, fish and many varieties of vegetables.

TRIBAL LIFE of banquets, dancing, praying and farming is seen in the picture of Secotan *(left)* near Roanoke. The rush mat sides of the huts could be rolled up for ventilation.

The indispensable buffalo,
basis of a civilization

BUFFALO, properly called bison, roamed more widely than is usually supposed, coming eastward as far as Georgia and Maryland. Before the Spaniards brought horses to America, buffalo were taken by stalking them on foot, by driving them into traps or by stampeding them over cliffs. After the Indians captured and learned to ride their first horses, an entire way of life was founded on buffalo killed by mounted hunters. Besides furnishing life's necessities in meat, clothes, moccasins, fuel and tent coverings, buffalo were powerful spirits; in the Indian religion, they could be angry or benevolent. They could teach medicine men how to cure the sick. The earliest picture of Indians hunting buffalo (*below*) is a detail from a 1595 map of New Spain (Mexico). But the best pictures of what the buffalo meant to Indians were made 250 years later by George Catlin, an American artist who devoted a lifetime to seeking out and recording the ways of those tribes which had least contact with Europeans. In 1832, Catlin painted Mandan life in North Dakota. Within a few years this tribe was almost wiped out by smallpox spread by incoming whites, and scenes like the one at right were ended forever.

INDIAN HUNTERS downing small buffalo are drawn out of scale in this 1595 sketch, probably based on a Spanish explorer's description of a scene in the southwestern plains.

BUFFALO DANCE, painted by Catlin (*right*), is meant to ensure fertility in the herds. Performers garbed as buffalo are watched by gaily dressed Mandan on rooftops.

An Iowa war party strides the prairies in the 1830s, silently and menacingly. Visible in Catlin's painting are scalp locks, prized trophies

Warriors and hunters of the Great Plains

TIRED TRIBESMAN on the upper Missouri relaxes in a steam bath. After cold water thrown on hot stones produced steam, the tepee was closed and the man rested amid reviving vapors.

THE Plains Indians had pleasures, even quite sensual indulgences, as the pictures to right and left show. But the core of their lives was war and hunting. This can be explained in economic terms: the Dakota tribes, familiarly known as the Sioux, fought to hold the best buffalo country in the upper Missouri basin not only against their historic foes, the Cree and Chippewa, but also against their own near relatives, the Assiniboin, Crow, Iowa, Omaha and Mandan. But Indians thought in non-economic terms. The young Dakota dreamed of captives and scalps that would bring him fame and glory in the tribe. So he fought Indians, white settlers and dashing General Custer, and earned such great renown that most Americans mean a Dakota tribesman when they say Indian. Little boys wear his magnificent, eagle-feathered war bonnet when they play cowboys and Indians, and men sometimes wear it, with some embarrassment, as one of the rites of American political campaigns.

for victors in tribal warfare. During the early 19th Century, the Iowa took many casualties in constant fighting with the powerful Dakota.

BATHING BRAVES in the Yellowstone River are Crow. The most elegant Indians, their tents and clothes were softer and whiter than those of any other tribe, and their bows were often elaborately covered with elk horn and rattlesnake skins. They wore their hair very long, frequently adding false hair to make it seem longer. And they were formidable in battle.

HAIDA LEADERS, in carved and painted masks with eyes and mouths that ingeniously open and close, perform the medicine mask dance of their tribe. This sacred ceremony, painted in 1847 by Paul Kane, preceded nearly every important activity in war or peace.

NISKA CRAFTSMEN of the northern region of British Columbia, using chisels of elk horn, stone mallets and shell scrapers, shape a felled tree to lines marked out by a master builder. In the 1850s, Catlin told of as many as 100 Niska working together on a job.

24

An affluent society with a taste for waste

AMONG the many Pacific Coast tribes, from Oregon to southern Alaska, the accumulation of wealth rather than the display of bravery was the business of life. Tribes lived in wood-planked mansions decorated with carved paneling and coats of arms. A class of artists grew up that made elaborate totem poles, canoes and masks. Tribe fought tribe for prisoners, and the most desirable prisoner was a skilled artist whose creations became the focal point of a strange ceremony, the potlatch. The word originally meant "gift-giving," but in the rite one chief would give away or even destroy all his possessions before the eyes of a rival chief. To save face, the second chief had to outdo the first chief. This kept the artists working busily to supply new treasures for destruction.

MOHAVE TRIBESMEN are shown in an 1858 painting. These handsome, fierce fighters of California often starved because they did not master the farming lore of their Pueblo neighbors.

MAGIC SHIELD of Chief Arapoosh, leader of the Montana Crow in the early 1800s, represents the moon in human form. The shield was spun, and its final position decided tribal problems.

Rituals of violence
for centuries of savage war

FOR all Indians the pursuit of war involved elaborate ritual. In some tribes, the young brave went off into the wilderness to fast and pray until his guardian spirit whispered to him the design he must paint on his shield and the song he must sing in combat or while dying. In other tribes, the warrior took emetics to purify himself for the fighting. Everywhere they painted themselves in colorful patterns and danced with their medicine men to obtain magical powers for battle; afterward, they danced to boast of their deeds.

The buffalo-hide shields and medicine men's shirts are now in museums. The war party slinking through the forest, the great herds of buffalo thundering over the plains with hunters on their flanks, live only in storybooks. But it took the white man 300 years of little sins and monstrous crimes to destroy the world of the Indian.

RITUAL SHIRT of an Apache medicine man (left) displays magic symbols believed by the Indians to incarnate special powers. But the spell appears to have failed; this shirt was captured in Arizona by an officer of the U.S. Cavalry in the 19th Century.

FIGHTING CHIEF of the Hidatsa tribe's elite Dog Society of warriors is seen in this 1833 painting by Karl Bodmer (right). Dancing out the story of his war exploits, he wears a feathery cap and around his neck a whistle made of a swan's wing bone.

2. AN ERA
OF EPOCHAL
DISCOVERY

A<small>T</small> sunrise, a pelican flew past the *Santa María*. The tiny squadron of three Spanish ships, according to the private reckoning which the admiral kept secret from his crew, was then some 2,100 miles west of the last landfall it had made three weeks before. On and off for the next week large flocks of birds, including ravens, were sighted by the restive men, a sure sign that land was near. One day, sailors on the *Pinta* saw a green branch floating by. Shortly afterward the *Niña's* crew fished out of the water a branch of thorns laden with red berries. The next morning, in the first faint light of dawn, a sailor on the *Pinta* called out *"Tierra! Tierra!* [Land! Land!]" The ship fired a lombard, her biggest piece of artillery. In a few hours the three ships anchored off a small island which Admiral Christopher Columbus named San Salvador, which in Spanish means "Blessed Savior."

On that day, October 12, 1492, the course of history was changed.

Columbus' voyage was not merely a stab into the unknown. True, it took colossal self-confidence, stout determination and superb nautical skill on the part of the leader of the expedition to reach the New World. Columbus had all these, but his voyage through uncharted seas was also based on a century of solid navigational achievements of many other Europeans. He was sailing into the unknown, but he was not sailing blindly.

Serious and systematic expansion of geographical knowledge by sailors and scholars had been sponsored from the early 15th Century by Prince Henry the

THE GREAT DISCOVERER is shown in the garb of an Italian Renaissance gentleman. This portrait was painted after Columbus' death, perhaps copied from a true likeness.

Navigator of Portugal, one of the greatest patrons of cosmography and exploration in history. Searching for a sea route to India, Portuguese explorers opened the western coast of Africa to Europeans. By 1488 Díaz had rounded the Cape of Good Hope. A decade later Vasco da Gama completed an extraordinary round-trip voyage to the Malabar coast of India.

Like Columbus, these men ventured farther and with greater safety than any who had sailed before them because of steady improvements in navigational instruments and knowledge. In the Middle Ages, European seamen finally came into possession of the magnetic compass to determine direction and the astrolabe to determine latitude. During the 15th Century the portolani, the first practical hydrographic charts, were improved and updated. Ship construction advanced by great leaps. The Portuguese caravel, with its broad bows, high, narrow poop and triangular lateen sails, was fast and could sail against the wind more efficiently than earlier ships.

Despite these advances, prodigies of navigational skill were still required of the seamen who ventured far offshore. The development of reliable chronometers and watches was far in the future, so it was difficult to determine longitude at sea. Mariners proceeded by sailing to the desired latitude and then turning onto the course they would hold until their goal was reached, estimating distance covered as best they could. Columbus, for example, sailed westward on the latitude of Japan, which was the goal he sought. On the way he was aided by northeast trade winds and by occasional helpful ocean currents. On his return trip, sailing a more northerly course, he was helped by the prevailing westerlies, of whose existence he was ignorant.

The monarchs of Portugal and Spain did not finance expeditions out of an enthusiasm for pure scientific information. They were prompted by a mixture of economic, religious and military motivations. They envied the trade monopoly that Venice and Genoa had carved out for themselves during the era of the Crusades from the Bosporus to the Strait of Gibraltar. From Arabia, India and China, profits came to fill the coffers of the Italian merchant princes. They imported goods which brought handsome prices in Europe: pepper, cinnamon, cloves and nutmeg; raw silk and cotton; oranges, medicaments,

: Xₚₒ FERENS./

A man fond of little secrets, Columbus signed his name in many special ways. Above he combined the Greek letters "Xρο" (Christ) with the Latin "ferens" (bearing) to produce Christopher (bearing Christ). His accurate map of the northwest of Hispaniola is shown below, against a modern map (in brown) of the same region, now Haiti and the Dominican Republic.

HISPANIOLA

dyestuffs and precious stones. Caravans brought these trade goods overland to Syrian ports; Italian traders moved them across the seas, through the passes of the Alps and on to the trading centers of northern Europe.

When the Portuguese opened the cheaper water route to the Orient around Africa, they shattered these traditional trade patterns. Their early voyages to the Indies broke the price of pepper in Venice and ended Venetian dominance of the spice trade. In the course of the century that followed, the main current of navigation and commerce shifted from the Mediterranean to the Atlantic. This shift, which had great financial and ultimately political significance, was part of what came to be known as the Commercial Revolution.

The Portuguese court gave Columbus no encouragement when he asked for backing to make his epic voyage. It was the Spanish monarchs, Ferdinand and Isabella, who agreed to sponsor his expedition. They did so as an act of national pride, for the province of Granada had recently been taken from its Moorish conquerors and Spain was now a consolidated Catholic nation. In supporting a voyage that aimed westward, rather than around Africa, the Spanish rulers were farsighted indeed. However, at the very moment that Columbus was raising sail, the Jews were being expelled from Spain. In pressing Columbus' exploration program, Spain took an enormous step forward; in expelling Jews as well as Moors, Spain ensured the eventual transience of its glory, for the technical, scientific and business skills of these people were never to be replaced in the country.

Columbus' flagship "Santa Maria" is shown in a 1493 engraving made in Spain to illustrate the official report of his discoveries. The artist never viewed the vessel, but Columbus probably approved the picture. This was his biggest vessel, but Columbus never liked his flagship. He thought it a dull sailer and was not greatly grieved when it was lost on Hispaniola.

MUCH of the documentation covering Christopher Columbus' early life is suspect in one way or the other, but it is now generally agreed that this Spanish-speaking navigator was born in Genoa. The Great Admiral's end was almost as obscure as his beginnings. Even his burial place has been a matter of dispute, and both the cathedrals at Santo Domingo in the West Indies and Seville in Spain claim to have his remains.

There is no mystery, though, about what Columbus achieved in seeking a westward route to "the Indies." In four voyages made between 1492 and 1504, he discovered and explored the northeastern coast of Cuba and the northern coast of Hispaniola, charted most of the Caribbean islands, sighted the northeast coast of South America; and finally, still in search of a route to the Indies, skirted the Honduran coast and explored as far as the present-day Gulf of Darien, off Panama. Nevertheless, he never realized that he had discovered a New World. To his dying day he stubbornly insisted that these lands were an extension of the Asian mainland. He declared that only a channel separated the West Indies he had found from "The Golden Chersonese [Malay Peninsula] of Ptolemy," and that "it was no farther from Panama to the Ganges than from Pisa to Genoa."

Columbus' reputation is, however, marred by his shortcomings as an administrator. During his rule of Hispaniola, the natives were cruelly exploited and his personal character was tarnished by rapacity.

To avoid a possible conflict between Spain and Portugal over the new lands, Pope Alexander VI in 1493 issued a bull grandly dividing the world. Spain was granted exclusive rights to the area 100 leagues (about 300 miles) west of the Azores and the Cape Verde Islands. The lands east of that line were reserved to Portugal. This arrangement recognized both Portugal's pre-eminent position in the waters east to India, and Spain's rigorous westward push. One

year later, by mutual agreement, the two powers moved the line of demarcation 370 leagues west of the Cape Verde Islands. Thus the land that was to become Brazil fell within Portugal's sphere six years before the Portuguese explorer Pedro Alvares Cabral reached its coast. The rest of the New World lay open to the exclusive exploitation of Spain.

For Spain and Portugal the division of the New World was a fine arrangement, but other nations disavowed it. The Italian known to history as John Cabot, voyaging for England's Henry VII, led two expeditions to the North Atlantic coast in 1497-1498. He ranged widely, from Cape Breton or Newfoundland in the north to as far south, possibly, as Chesapeake Bay. A Florentine merchant and banker named Amerigo Vespucci in the same period participated in several expeditions which explored more than two thirds of the eastern coastline of South America. Vespucci's reputation as a serious explorer was to suffer from exaggerated accounts of his achievements. But his claim that he had "arrived at a new land which . . . we observed to be a continent" led the geographer Martin Waldseemüller to propose in 1507 that the newly discovered world should be called the "land of Americus, for Americus its discoverer." And thus the New World came to be named.

As successive voyages more clearly delineated the lands Columbus had found, it became apparent that they were indeed a vast New World and a great land barrier to the Indies. In 1513 Vasco Núñez de Balboa crossed the Isthmus of Panama and from a mountain peak perceived the limitless reaches of the Pacific, whose existence Europeans had not suspected. Ferdinand Magellan was the first European to sail upon it. An accomplished Portuguese navigator and geographer who was out of favor with his own court and was therefore sponsored by Charles I of Spain, Magellan proved that there was a western water route to the Indies. On his epochal voyage in 1519-1521 he rounded the southern tip of South America through the treacherous cliff-bordered strait that now bears his name, and brought his ships all the way to Guam and finally to the Philippines, where he died protecting the retreat of a landing party under attack by hostile natives. In 1522, Juan Sebastián del Cano, a subaltern of Magellan, completed the circumnavigation of the globe Magellan had begun. The three-year voyage demonstrated that the world was indeed round, and measured its circumference. It also proved that the other side of the earth was habitable, a discovery that Spain was to exploit later in the 16th Century when she colonized the Philippines.

MORE immediately, however, the Spaniards concentrated on the conquest —and looting—of Central and South America. Hernán Cortés took Mexico from the Aztec in 1521 and sent its glittering treasures of gold to Spain. In a savage nine-year campaign, Francisco Pizarro conquered the Peruvian-centered empire of the Inca with its even greater riches in silver. The resultant flood of precious metals into Europe precipitated a price revolution, during which prices rose more than 100 per cent in Spain. The vast increase in the quantity of money transformed western European society. The feudal structure was weakened, the insecurity of the working class was increased, capitalist activity was spurred and the less wealthy nations were aroused. Moreover, the expanded supply of money paid for the European conquest of the Americas as well as the transportation and resettlement of countless emigrants from the teeming Old World to the empty spaces of the New.

For years Amerigo Vespucci was an agent for the princely merchant house of the Medici, which traded in such things as buttermilk curds, pigeons and mulberry seed. Then, aged 45, he left the countinghouse for the sea, explored the new hemisphere discovered by Columbus, and lived to see it named America.

Hernando de Soto was rich, handsome and, as a contemporary said, "fond of this sport of killing Indians." On his march from Florida he took along 13 hogs, which bred so rapidly that at the end of three years the leader's share alone was 700. He also collected Indian women, and at one time he had six.

Encouraged by these rich initial rewards, Spain explored and claimed vast stretches of the Americas, notably along the Gulf of Mexico and the Atlantic coastline. Ponce de León explored Florida in 1513 and returned to that peninsula again in 1521. Lucas Vázquez de Ayllón investigated the Carolina coast, and in 1524-1525 the Portuguese Esteban Gómez surveyed the Atlantic Coast still farther north. But the Spaniards wanted no part of the colder regions. They left it to their impatient rivals, the French, the English and the Dutch, to develop what they considered not worth exploiting.

In the South and Southwest of the American continent, the Spaniards established claims that were to go unchallenged for many years. Hernando de Soto reached the Mississippi in 1541 after an arduous journey from the Florida coast into Georgia, across the Great Smokies into Tennessee and southwest almost to the Gulf of Mexico. He crossed the mighty river to reconnoiter the Ozark country, and pressed as far west as Oklahoma before he returned to the Mississippi to die of a fever in 1542. Even earlier, Cabeza de Vaca traveled across Texas and New Mexico to Arizona. Francisco Vázquez de Coronado led a force into New Mexico to conquer the fabled Seven Cities of Cíbola. He found no cities, but he returned to Mexico City in 1542 with a fund of fascinating data about the interior of the continent.

O THER explorers meanwhile carried the flag of Spain up the Pacific Coast, to a point just below the present California-Oregon border. Permanent settlement was not undertaken there, however, until the very eve of the American Revolution, when a system of military posts and Franciscan missions, the latter under the inspired leadership of Fray Junípero Serra, was established at San Diego, Monterey, San Francisco and elsewhere. This late Spanish spurt into California was stimulated by concern about the threat of Russian expansion down the northwest Pacific Coast. Vitus Bering, a Danish explorer working for the Russian government, had already crossed the strait which bears his name and probed the Aleutians and the coast of Alaska. Spain also feared the possibility of English expansion westward from the Atlantic coastal colonies, the Ohio Valley or Canada.

The settlement of California was the final act in Spain's systematic conquest of America. By the time the French and English began colonizing, Spain had established permanent settlements in Florida and also in the Southwest, which Juan de Oñate first settled in 1598. In these areas, as later on the Pacific Coast, the aim was not loot, but labor. The tasks of rendering the Indians obedient and of organizing the labor force in permanent villages were entrusted largely to the missionaries in the villages and to the proprietors of the great cattle ranches. Despite the fact that Florida and the Southwest produced little wealth for the empire and held only a marginal interest for the home government, Spain tenaciously held its outposts in these borderlands for over two centuries. The vastly richer heartland in Central and South America remained Spanish for over 325 years. This was almost as long as the sway of imperial Rome over western Europe, and longer than the British hold over the American colonies or India. Self-government as it was known in the English colonies was never granted to Spain's American possessions. But that sort of self-government was unknown in Spain itself. The Spanish colonies remained technically under the centralized control of viceroys, subject to check in varying degrees by the *audiencia,* or royal colonial council.

A haughty Portuguese, Ferdinand Magellan was a strict disciplinarian. On his voyage around South America at the head of a five-ship fleet he viciously punished one mutinous captain after another. He had one skinned alive, a second stabbed in the heart, a third put in chains and a fourth marooned.

Before Ponce de León went to seek eternal youth in Florida, he brutally "pacified" the Indians of Puerto Rico with the help of a savage dog, Bercerillo. "The Indians," noted a writer, "were more afraid of ten Spaniards with the dog than of 100 without." Ponce allotted part of the plunder on the dog's behalf.

The Spaniards left no heritage of freedom, but they did leave a permanent cultural imprint. They brought printing presses and universities to the New World a century before the English. We see the Spanish heritage today in the Castillo de San Marcos in Saint Augustine, in San Antonio's inspired San José Mission and in countless other missions in the Southwest, in regional festivals and the rodeo. Spain is stamped on the Texas homestead law, on mining and water laws, and on community property arrangements of the American Southwest. And in some southwestern communities a politician still wins votes by addressing his constituents in Spanish.

Jacques Cartier, a shipmaster of Saint-Malo, offered the Indians hardtack and red wine when he first explored the St. Lawrence region in 1534 and 1535. As a result the Indians insisted the French ate wood and drank blood. But they reacted more favorably to French guns, for which they traded furs.

WHILE the Spaniards were exploiting the Americas for gold and silver, the English and the French amassed less glamorous wealth. They found fish in unparalleled abundance off Newfoundland and the North Atlantic shores, and developed a thriving commerce which provided food for Spain and much of Catholic Europe. Where the fishermen set up temporary stations ashore to dry their catch, they began trading with the Indians for furs, and the fur trade gradually grew into a business that led France in the 17th Century to send out explorers who penetrated the interior of the continent.

Earlier, in 1534, the Frenchman Jacques Cartier made a reconnaissance of Newfoundland, and in the following year he sailed up the St. Lawrence. Searching for a passage to China or for rich empires like Mexico and Peru, he also sought to consolidate the claims to the northeastern coast which Verrazano, the discoverer of New York in 1524, had made for Francis I. Cartier returned with nothing to show the king for his efforts but "false gold," probably copper or iron pyrites. The French did not press further exploration until 1603, when Henry IV supported an expedition to the St. Lawrence. Samuel de Champlain, who had served as the expedition's cartographer, returned to France with beaver skins and tales of vast lakes far up the St. Lawrence, past many rapids and a great waterfall. Subsequently, Champlain made a number of trips in eastern Canada—11 in all—on which he combined exploration and trade. He erected a trading post at Quebec in 1608, and in 1609 he ventured up a river into the lake in New York State named after him. He saw at once the possibilities of the fur trade. Shrewdly, he established friendly relations with the Algonquin and joined the Huron in inconclusive raids against their ancient enemies, the Iroquois.

No less significant were the exploits of Médard Chouart, Sieur des Groseilliers, who in 1654-1656, still pursuing the dream of "a river which empties into . . . the China Sea," reached Lake Michigan. He and his brother-in-law Pierre Radisson initiated fur-trading agreements in areas never before penetrated by the eastern traders. After them came the colorful *coureurs de bois*, the loose-living, ribald, wilderness-loving traders who called on the Indians in the back reaches and, fortified with daring and brandy in about equal amounts, swapped liquor for furs.

Samuel de Champlain, founder of French Canada, was a hardheaded, shrewd soldier, but he was also gullible. When a fun-loving officer told him of a Bay of Fundy monster twice as tall as a ship that ate Indians while letting out horrible noises, he thought there was probably a good deal of truth in it.

Later on, Groseilliers and Radisson broke with France over a question of taxation. Under the flag of England, these daring men explored the vast Hudson Bay area, and helped found the Hudson's Bay Company, England's great fur-trading combine.

New France was at first administered by companies of merchants holding royal grants, but in 1664 the colonies passed under the direct supervision of the crown. Under Louis XIV, the territories were ruled by a governor, usually

a nobleman sent from the homeland, and an intendant, next to the governor in dignity but somewhat above him in real authority. Church affairs were supervised by a bishop. The most dynamic figure in the early history of the areas that came to be known as Canada was a handsome Gascon soldier of commanding presence, the Count de Frontenac, who was made governor in 1672. A man with many ideas of his own, he was recalled in 1682 because his advocacy of a representative assembly for the colony and his approval of brandy as barter for furs were directly opposed to policies of the crown and the church. But in 1689, when the French colonial empire was threatened by the English and their Indian allies, he was sent back at the age of 69 and succeeded in repulsing an English attack upon Quebec.

While new colonies slowly grew in Canada, France pressed on with exploration of the continent's interior. Louis Joliet, a fur trader born in Quebec, teamed with the Jesuit scholar Father Marquette, master of many Indian languages, to journey westward through Lake Michigan and Lake Winnebago, then down the Wisconsin River to the Mississippi. They stopped at the mouth of the Arkansas River. Joliet returned to Quebec early in 1674 to report that the Mississippi was a route to the Gulf of Mexico and not to the "Vermilion Sea," as the Gulf of California was then known because of its reddish color. That 2,500-mile, four-month canoe trip opened up for France the great central watershed of the continent. By the same route Robert Cavelier, Sieur de la Salle, in 1682 reached the mouth of the Mississippi, where he claimed "this country of Louisiana" for Louis XIV. Thus France began the settlement of both extremes of the Mississippi.

The Illinois country was peopled by farmers, who shipped their grain downriver to New Orleans. The fledgling port, founded in 1718, exported rice, indigo, tobacco and some cotton both to the upstream settlements and to markets abroad. In contrast with Louisiana, French Canada lacked a balanced economy. It had practically no manufactures, and its people neglected farming for the quicker rewards from hunting and the fur trade.

When fur trader Louis Joliet and Jesuit Father Jacques Marquette (standing) explored the Mississippi River by canoe they encountered many huge catfish, one of which, the priest reported, "struck our Canoe with such violence that I Thought that it was a great tree, about to break the Canoe to pieces."

CULTURALLY, New France lagged behind both the Spanish and the English colonies: no newspaper or book was printed there until the mid-18th Century. And since the crown never put its full influence behind an active program of settlement, the French colonies were never adequately populated. By 1763 they had barely managed to settle some 80,000 people from Canada to Louisiana, a stretch of territory more than 2,000 miles in length. In a much more circumscribed area, the English colonies had 1.8 million settlers who grew to 2.5 million by the time of the American Revolution in 1776.

Nonetheless, in spite of wars and ultimate conquest by the British, the French of Canada remained doggedly French in orientation. To this day, areas in the province of Quebec are reminiscent of 17th Century France in speech and custom, and Canada is officially bilingual. In the United States the marriage of French and Spanish cultures where the two imperial powers overlapped in Louisiana resulted in a cultural blend known as Creole, reflected in the French Quarter of New Orleans, known as the Vieux Carré. There, narrow streets and buildings of a distinctive style, with patios and intricate wrought-iron balconies, are reminders that all of Louisiana's colonial history was spent under the flags of France and Spain.

In the century after Columbus, no nation in Europe underwent a greater

transformation than England. In 1492, the English were still a nation of shepherds and farmers, just emerging from the paralyzing dynastic Wars of the Roses. England had no maritime power, and in any case its Tudor kings were too concerned with domestic problems to think of vying with Spain in the New World. Spanish initiative did awaken feelings of envy and regret among Englishmen, but at that particular time England was not prepared to do anything about it.

I T was trade rather than colonization that put England on the road to greatness. Its woolen cloth was its most valuable manufacture, and there were innumerable customers abroad for this quality product if England could only reach them. So shipbuilders created an English merchant fleet (to the detriment of Venice, which formerly had carried the island's goods), and to protect it a fledgling navy emerged. English companies dispatched English woolen goods in English merchant vessels to the Baltic and Russia, to the Near East and even to the East Indies.

This was making money in a sure and comparatively safe way. It was not comparable to the quick riches won by Spain in Peru and Mexico, but it created a solid base for power. By the time Elizabeth ascended the throne in 1558, England was ready for a golden age. Inspired equally by the fervor of militant Protestantism and a new sense of national goals—as well as plain envy—the English began to attack Spanish naval power while nominally remaining at peace with Spain.

The first stage of the worldwide maritime rivalry introduced the "sea dog," or privateer, an independent soldier-sailor-entrepreneur who dealt in casks of sugar and butts of wine as well as with great affairs of state. John Hawkins was one of the early sea dogs. At the same time that he was systematically raiding Spain's Caribbean ports, he was bringing African slaves to sell to the Spanish sugar planters there. His young cousin Francis Drake, whose audacity quickly won him the nickname of "The Dragon" among his foes, pressed these forays into the heart of the Spanish empire. In 1578 he took the *Golden Hind* through the Strait of Magellan into the Pacific, where he staged a spectacular raid on Spanish treasure ships. He went on to explore the California coast and anchored somewhere there, probably in San Francisco Bay, to refit his ship for the voyage across the Pacific. After obtaining a precious spice cargo in the Moluccas, Drake navigated the treasure-laden *Golden Hind* back to England in 1580. Queen Elizabeth knighted him for this exploit, in the full knowledge that this might be interpreted by the Spaniards as an overtly hostile act. Martin Frobisher's three voyages in search of a "Northwest Passage" had already enlarged British knowledge of the remoter reaches of northeastern Canada and of the sea Frobisher believed washed the northern part of America.

The daring and lucrative forays of the sea dogs demonstrated that England's small and highly maneuverable ships could successfully harass the mighty Spanish galleons. Thus ended Spain's long-established control of the sea lanes, and the time was ripe for a permanent English colony in America. Sir Humphrey Gilbert obtained a patent in 1578 "to inhabit and possess at his choice all remote and heathen lands not in the possession of any Christian Prince." He made two voyages of exploration in 1578 and 1583, but failed to persuade his men to remain as farmers in bleak and fogbound Newfoundland.

Giovanni Caboto (called John Cabot by his English employers) sailed from Bristol in 1497 on commission "to seeke out . . . regions . . . of the heathen." He made a landfall in Canada, laid claim to the region and hurried home, where the delighted king rewarded him with £10 "to have a good time with."

After Gilbert died, his projects were taken up by his half brother, the dashing and talented Sir Walter Raleigh. Dreaming of an English empire in the West, Raleigh wrote of America: "I shall yet live to see it an Inglishe nation." He laid his plans with care, choosing a southern route in preference to the one tried by his half brother, and he secured substantial financial backing in addition to making a heavy investment of his own.

In 1584 and 1585 Raleigh sponsored two trips to America. The land that was settled was named "Virginia" in honor of Elizabeth, the Virgin Queen. Raleigh was no more successful than Gilbert in establishing a permanent colony. The paintings of Indians and wildlife by John White excited considerable interest back in England, but Raleigh was hard put to assemble a third expedition, this one led by White. A landing was made at Roanoke Island in 1587. White returned to England for supplies, and it was three years before he saw Roanoke again. England was by now finally and fully involved in a life-and-death struggle with Spain, and had no resources to expend on such remote outposts as the small settlement in Virginia. When White at last came back to Roanoke, he found only some abandoned chests and the word "Croatoan" carved on a tree, suggesting that the colonists may have fled to a nearby island of that name. But not a single survivor was ever found. What happened at Roanoke remains one of the mysteries of early America.

Despite these early failures at settlement in the New World, the British were soon to dominate the colonial scene. The defeat of the Spanish Armada sent to invade England in 1588 damaged Spanish prestige throughout the world and tremendously weakened Spanish power at home and in the empire. The naval victory of the British encouraged bolder overseas ventures in settlement and brought closer the day when Englishmen would build for themselves a new life in the New World.

Sir Francis Drake, England's great fighting sailor, stormed and sacked Spanish towns all over the Americas but never neglected the niceties. "He is served on silver dishes with gold borders and gilded garlands, in which are his arms," reported a prisoner, "[and] he carries all possible dainties and perfumed waters."

M ANIFOLD and decisive were the consequences of England's entry upon the stage of colonization. On the eve of the Spanish Armada's ill-fated expedition against England, Philip II of Spain, to which Portugal was then joined, ruled all the permanent European settlements in the New World. A century later the English had entrenched themselves along the North Atlantic coast from Maine to the Carolinas, as well as in the Caribbean, and a goodly part of North America was forever lost to Spanish domination. Bit by bit, the rest of its holdings were to fall from its grasp.

Had the story been otherwise, had the Duke of Medina Sidonia, the Spanish admiral, triumphed over Howard, Hawkins and Drake in the narrow waters of the English Channel, had Spanish soldiers set foot in England, the character and history of North America most certainly would have taken on an entirely different shape. Its culture would have been Latin, not English; its religion Catholic, not Protestant; its native races would have been exploited rather than ejected; its colonies would have been controlled by the centralized Spanish government rather than allowed to form a group of quasi-independent, self-governing commonwealths. In short, the impulse toward freedom would have been checked, if not throttled. And it is inconceivable that revolution against a Spanish ruler, when and if it finally came, would have offered the shining example of a stable and flourishing republic built upon the Anglo-American tradition of constitutional rights, representative government and civil liberties.

Sir Humphrey Gilbert, maladroit mariner who was Sir Walter Raleigh's half brother, sailed to America despite a staggering series of mishaps. He lost some of his vessels on rocks, inadvertently signed pirates on his crews, lost a cargo in a storm and drowned when his ship sank on the way home.

Coronado's portrait, based on contemporary accounts.

"They spent three days on this bank looking for a passage down to the river.... It was impossible to descend.... What seemed to be easy from above was not so, but instead very hard and difficult."

THE GRAND CANYON of the Colorado *(opposite)* stuns the imagination and tricks the senses. Coronado's troops, who came upon it during a side trip, thought that some rocks on the canyon walls were as high as a man. But three men who got part way down reported that the rocks were taller than Seville cathedral's 275-foot bell tower.

An amazing journey to disillusion

EUROPEANS of the century after Columbus could scarcely guess what monsters, what fearsome hazards they might encounter in the vastnesses of America. Every early explorer saw at least something breathtaking, but few expeditions found so much that was new as did the one led by the Spaniard Francisco Vázquez de Coronado from 1540 to 1542. And few of the other expeditions covered more ground: from Mexico through Lower California to Kansas. The lure of treasure spurred Coronado, then 30, and his 336 conquistadors to their long trek. These were ruthless, greedy men whose unsurpassed courage in meeting setbacks was paired with deep piety; they took along a group of friars to convert the heathen. There were also hundreds of Indian scouts and servants, and herds of horses, mules, cattle and sheep. Horses from these and other Spanish herds revolutionized Indian life.

The journal kept by Pedro de Castañeda, from which the italicized quotations on these pages are taken, relates that Coronado returned a broken man, disappointed by his failure to find gold. He had seen sights similar to those pictured here, but had not been overly impressed. And he never realized he had found a far richer empire than any he had ever dared dream of.

A country of wonders: wine from spiny trees, "lions" and "leopards" high in the hills

"In . . . Vacapan there was a large quantity of prickly pears, of which the natives make a great deal of preserves. . . . As the men of the army ate much of it, they all fell sick with a headache and fever. . . ."

GAUNT SAGUARO cactus, at left, often reaching a height of 50 feet, is a kind of "thistle" like those mentioned in Castañeda's journal. Its juice is used to make a potent liquor; its fruit, together with the prickly pear, is still a favorite preserve of the Indians of the Southwest. It was pear preserve that Coronado's men ate with such bad results when they visited Vacapan, a village in Mexico.

"There are barbels and picones [catfish], like those of Spain, in the rivers. . . . Gray lions and leopards were seen. The country rises . . . from the beginning of the wilderness until Cibola is reached. . . ."

MOUNTAIN LIONS, or puma, still roam the mountains of the Southwest. In his chronicle of Coronado's expedition, Castañeda called them "gray lions." Those "leopards" were wildcats. Despite innumerable tall tales, both animals are shy of humans and rarely, if ever, attack them. The Pecos River, which Castañeda especially praised for its "very good trout and otters," remains noted for its fishing.

Strange storms, cliff-top villages and religious rituals

"A dry snow . . . fell all night long, covering the baggage and the soldiers. . . . Horses stood half buried in it. It kept those . . . underneath [it] warm instead of cold."

SNOW ON THE DESERT surrounds a clump of Joshua trees *(left)*. Castañeda also told of a very cold tornado and hailstones "as big as bowls, or bigger." His interest was also aroused by the Indians' "bread of the mesquite, like cheese, which keeps good for a whole year."

"The village was very strong . . . up on a rock out of reach, having steep sides in every direction, and so high that it was a very good musket that could throw a ball as high."

THE PUEBLO OF ACOMA stands isolated on a mesa *(below, right)* east of Zuni, New Mexico. This is the oldest continuously inhabited settlement in the U.S. It still looks much as it did when Coronado saw it. The Indians here, hostile at first, later became very friendly.

"In this country there were also tame eagles, which the chiefs esteemed. . . . There are a great many native fowl . . . and cocks with great hanging chins."

A GOLDEN EAGLE displays its seven-foot spread of wing *(left)*. Among the Pueblo Indians, especially the Zuñi and Hopi, feathers of eagles and turkeys with "hanging chins" were prized for solemn rites.

Sheep on the mountainsides; ceremonial rooms underground

"The men . . . saw a flock of sheep one day. . . . They had extremely large bodies and long wool; their horns were very thick and large, and when they run they throw back their heads. . . . They are used to the rough country . . . we could not catch them. . . ."

BIGHORN SHEEP, spectacular climbers and leapers *(above)*, range from Canada to Mexico. Though they average only about 40 inches high at the shoulder, they seemed to Coronado, as he reported in a letter sent to the viceroy of Mexico, to be as big as horses.

"They saw the largest and finest hot rooms or estufas that there were in the entire country, for they had a dozen pillars, each . . . twice as large around as one could reach and twice as tall as a man. . . . Some that were seen were large enough for a game of ball."

A RUINED KIVA of the pueblo of Braba, near modern Taos, New Mexico, stands behind domed ovens *(opposite)*. Called estufas by the Spaniards, the kivas were underground ceremonial chambers and male clubrooms open to women only for certain duties.

Memories of endless prairies

"As these [buffalo] fled they trampled one another in their haste until they came to a ravine. So many . . . fell into this that they filled it up, and the rest went across on top of them. The men who were chasing them on horseback fell in among the animals. . . . Three of the horses that fell in . . . were lost sight of completely."

THE VAST HERDS of "cows" with "very long beards" of Coronado's time are now reduced to small flocks like those seen below, fenced in game preserves. The springy grass that nourished the buffalo showed no mark of the Spaniards' passing as they hopefully chased the dream of the Seven Cities to the final disillusion of thatched huts on the Kansas plains. Though they returned with hopes crushed, the explorers carried glowing memories to their graves. After 20 years, Castañeda still vividly recalled the great prairies, "so level and smooth that . . . even if a man only lay down on his back he lost sight of the ground."

3. THE SOUTHERN PLANTATIONS

ONE day in December of 1606, a little over a hundred Englishmen crowded onto three small ships, the *Susan Constant, Godspeed* and *Discovery*, and set sail from London for what one of the men hopefully called "Virginia, Earth's only paradise." Many were gentlemen-adventurers. There were also four boys, 20 laborers and four carpenters—but no women—in this motley company moving down the Thames. Four storm-tossed months later, they entered hospitable Chesapeake Bay, and a month afterward finally anchored in the calm waters of the James River (so named in honor of King James I).

Their first impressions were exhilarating. They found, one of their number related, "fair meadows and goodly tall trees, with such fresh waters running through the woods as I was almost ravished with the first site thereof." Looking for an easily defensible site, the sea-weary voyagers pitched their tents on marshy and unhealthful ground, and soon famine and pestilence took a fearful toll. The long sea voyage had used up most of their provisions. As the first year neared its end, only 38 of the 104 were still alive in Jamestown.

It was a sorry beginning for the settlers, and the company that financed them finally went bankrupt. Yet a permanent English settlement in North America had at last been begun. And despite the frustrations and sacrifices that marked the first outposts at Jamestown and Plymouth, Englishmen could not be discouraged from emigrating to America in increasing numbers.

Why did they come, and why did they keep coming? Sir Walter Raleigh said

QUEEN ELIZABETH I, in whose ebullient reign was launched the momentous colonization of North America, carried from a state function by nobles of her court.

that it was "to seek new worlds for gold, for praise, for glory." Gold was certainly on the minds of the Jamestown settlers. One of the original company, Captain John Smith, records in his *Generall Historie of Virginia* that there was "no talke, no hope, nor worke, but dig gold, wash gold, refine gold, load gold." But no gold was found in Virginia. And not all the settlers were romantics in quest of praise and glory. There were, of course, adventurers whose patriotism was aroused by the defeat of the Spanish Armada. They were encouraged by the English government, which felt colonies would heighten its prestige. A ballad of the time, inspired by news of an early voyage to Virginia, expressed England's aspirations:

> Wee hope to plant a nation
> Where none before hath stood.

Tales of discovery, of the exploration of exotic lands, of victories over the hated Spaniards had fired the imagination of people of every class. These glowing visions were often sufficient to induce noblemen and the country gentry to desert their firesides for the perils of the Atlantic crossing.

But more personal motives were ordinarily needed to bestir the rank and file of emigrants. They were weavers, tradesmen, laborers. Among them was more than a liberal sprinkling of vagrants, paupers, orphans, pickpockets and women of the streets who came to Virginia to start life anew, to escape the degradation and hopelessness that had been their lot in the mother country.

Many of the emigrants were farmers who came to acquire cheap or free land. For the yeomen freeholders, the small farmers of England, the times were out of joint. Sheep raising on a large scale had been started toward the end of the 15th Century to meet the needs of England's growing export trade in wool. To create broad grazing areas, Parliament enacted laws authorizing the enclosure, or fencing off, of the narrow strips in various parts of the common land which had been allotted in medieval times for tillage. In return for his loss of his tilling privilege on common land, the farmer received a single

JAMES I (1603-1625)

When James Stuart, King of Scotland, succeeded his cousin Queen Elizabeth, he became the first of many English rulers who left their imprint on the American colonies. Learning that a band of Puritan emigrants planned to become fishermen, James exclaimed in delight, ". . . the Apostles' own calling."

CHARLES I (1625-1649)

Charles, the shy, defensive son of James I, engaged in a long, losing struggle for power with Parliament. First many of his opponents, and later many of his supporters, sought a refuge in the colonies. Place names like the Charles River and Charlestown in Massachusetts recall his tumultuous reign.

CROMWELL (1653-1658)

Oliver Cromwell rose from obscurity in Parliament to rule England with more power than had the deposed king. While he introduced reforms at home, his Puritan revolt substituted parliamentary for Royalist control of the colonial governments, temporarily increasing the colonies' independence of action.

CHARLES II (1660-1685)

Charles was a relief to England after its two exhausting decades of Puritanism. He made an elegant king and, heeding the lesson of his beheaded father, deferred to Parliament. Colonial commerce expanded in spite of his Navigation Acts, and Charleston, South Carolina, bears his royal name.

farm. But on balance, he was generally a loser in this redistribution. The plot he was given was usually poorer and smaller than the land he had formerly used. It was worse for the many farmers who did not own their land as free-holders but worked it as tenants. They had only hereditary claims as descendants of villeins, or servile tenants, and lost their lands completely because they could not show technical title. "Sheep eat men" was the bitter cry of the evicted. Sir Edward Coke, commenting on the decline of the countryside and the growth of vagrancy, denounced the "de-populator who turns all out of doors and keeps none but a shepherd and his dog." Riots broke out in England over the enclosures in the very year that Jamestown was settled.

Another device called rack renting intensified hardships of English country people in the late 16th and early 17th Centuries. The landlords now argued with pitiless logic that the old and traditional rents, based on medieval values of land, were unrealistic. Accordingly, they boosted rents of tenant farmers several hundred per cent. And while rents and prices rose rapidly, the wages of farm laborers were held down. These wages had for centuries been set by the country justices of the peace, themselves large landowners who were naturally conservative about granting wage rises. A worker earned little more in the reign of James I than he had a century earlier in the days of Henry VIII.

The new scarcity of land and the spread of unemployment and vagrancy fostered the notion that England was overpopulated. This furnished another stimulus to colonization. And enthusiasm for emigration was further supported in the early years of settlement by the widely held theory that if the unemployed and vagrant classes were shipped to the colonies, they could produce the raw materials needed at home and at the same time consume England's surplus of manufactures. Thus resettlement was warmly encouraged by the merchant capitalists whose ideology has been loosely labeled mercantilism.

To some degree, all of the colonizing powers subscribed to mercantilist notions. Although they disagreed on details, all mercantilists believed in building self-sufficient national states or empires. They argued that a sizable state

JAMES II (1685-1688)

Lacking the imagination and caution of his brother Charles II, James had one consistent policy—to have his own way. Within four years he had to flee before a foreign king invited to England to maintain English liberties. New York was named for James while he was its lord as Duke of York.

WILLIAM III (1689-1702)

When the king of Holland accepted England's crown, he agreed not to act independently of Parliament. Thus the "glorious" revolution ended the "divine right" of English kings. William's reliance on ministers hastened the growth of political parties. Williamsburg, Virginia, was named after him.

MARY II (1689-1694)

Mary was cursed by her deposed father James II when she and her husband William took the throne. Her popularity aided William's early reign. Despite his cold reserve, she loved him with "a passion that cannot end but with my life." Both were ended by smallpox a few years after she was crowned.

ANNE (1702-1714)

Anne, the last and most ordinary of the Stuarts, succeeded the husband of her childless sister Mary. While annexation enlarged Britain's empire, Anne entrusted her policies to a series of favorites, notably the Duke of Marlborough. Annapolis, which became Maryland's capital, was named for her.

treasury was required to maintain a nation's security forces in readiness. Gold and silver would flow into the treasury if the nation sold more abroad than it bought. To ensure such a favorable balance of payments, tariff walls against imports had to be erected, and domestic producers had to be bolstered by ensuring them essential raw materials and low production costs.

Mercantilism implied a dual role for the colonies, whose interests must always be subordinate to the mother country's. First, colonies proved their worth when they furnished products the mother country had previously been compelled to buy from foreign, often enemy, nations. For England, these products would be timber and naval stores for the Royal Navy, until then purchased from Baltic lands; silks from Italy and France; sugar and spices from several distant places. Second, colonies should mean expanding markets for such English products as cloth, nails and other hardware.

The English merchant capitalists who invested in colonizing projects believed that their pursuit of profit also served the national welfare. Their philosophy was summed up by the poet and cleric John Donne in a sermon preached to the Virginia Company in London in 1622. Donne pointed out that while cash profits were still distant, the Virginia plantation already was returning dividends of another sort. "It shall redeem many a wretch from the jaws of death, from the hands of the executioner. . . . It shall sweep your streets and wash your doors from idle persons and the children of idle persons, and employ them." Indeed, Donne pointed out, Virginia was more than "a spleen to drain ill humours of the body." It was already breeding a fine, new kind of Englishman, and providing employment for mariners and profits on maritime freight. It had already become "a mark for the envy and for the ambition of our enemies."

D ESPITE the discontents at home which had led many of them to face the perils of the Atlantic crossing and the tomahawk of the Indian, the early colonists continued to think of the mother country with deep affection. So it was natural for the colonists to reproduce in the wilderness many of the institutions of government they had known at home. As the American poet Stephen Vincent Benét has put it:

> And those who came were resolved to be Englishmen,
> Gone to the World's end, but English every one,
> And they ate the white corn-kernels, parched in the sun
> And they knew it not, but they'd not be English again.

The evolution of the transplanted political institutions is the central theme of colonial history, for the changes that occurred contained the germ of the later movement for independence from England.

The average settler came from a village or a small town where he had known his local officials at first hand. He knew, first of all, the parish that supported the church, administered poor relief and checked on morals, and he knew the vestrymen or churchwardens who ran the parish. In earlier times, the vestry had been elected by all the parishioners, but by the 17th Century, a few of the most influential local citizens controlled the selection. When parishes were established in Virginia, they followed the English model.

Similarly, the colonists used the English model in adapting that other bulwark of English local government, the country justices. In Virginia, these

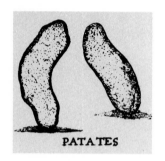

PATATES

The common potato, shown above in an early drawing, reached Europe from South America by the 1550s, and Englishmen took it to Virginia in 1621. Tobacco (below), the "bewitching vegetable" smoked by the Indians, became a fashionable habit. But when Walter Raleigh's servant first saw him smoking, he drenched his master with water to save him from burning.

were called county commissioners and were appointed by the governor. County government was well suited to the scattered rural communities of early Virginia, as it later was to the rest of the South. The commissioner or squire, though a layman, often knew as much about statutes as about soils. He settled petty civil quarrels, judged criminal cases short of those involving life and limb, supervised road construction and repair, and set prices for services and products where a public interest was involved.

I N addition to the apparatus of local government, the English settlers brought with them certain concepts of constitutional government and civil liberties that distinguished them from all of the other European colonists. To "live as free English men," asserted Virginia's governing council, was to live "under the government of just and equall lawes, and not as a slave after the will and lust of any superiour." The first settlers in Virginia, like most Englishmen, considered their king to be subject to the law, even though James I was just then claiming to rule by divine right. These Virginians, in similar proportions as their kinsmen at home, applauded Parliament's increasing assertion of the people's rights, its demands for complete control over legislation and taxation, its insistence on freedom from arbitrary imprisonment, and its assertion of the right of petition. The 17th Century in England was the time when Parliament established its supremacy over the king. The 18th Century in the colonies was to witness a power struggle between the colonial assemblies, whose aspirations reflected the victories of Parliament at home and the royal authority in the persons of the governors.

The powers of the crown in Virginia were somewhat limited by the fact that it had not itself initiated the settlement of the colony. It is important to recall that this had been done by a joint stock company, a venture in which investors pooled their capital and shared the risks of a business. This kind of company had been active in domestic and foreign enterprises for half a century. Two such organizations were chartered by the crown in 1606: the Virginia Company consisted of London entrepreneurs who planned a settlement in the southern part of Virginia, and the Plymouth Company, made up of West Country people who proposed to develop northern Virginia. Once a company had made its selection of sites, it was granted the land extending 50 miles north and south of the original settlement and 100 miles inland.

Under the 1606 charters, the governmental powers were divided between a royal council resident in England and a local council in the colony. But this division of command between crown and company, and between absentee governors and on-the-spot councilors, quickly proved impractical. A new charter given the Virginia Company in 1609 transferred the entire responsibility of government from the crown to the company. It also granted an equal share in profits to the stockholders in England who invested money and the planters in the colony who contributed labor. The charter enlarged the grant to include all land 200 miles north and south of Old Point Comfort, not far from Jamestown, and extending west and northwest to the Pacific Ocean. (This extravagant donation, based on vague notions about the size of the continent, was the basis of Virginia's later claim to the Northwest Territory, as well as to the wilderness west of the mountains.) Three years later, in 1612, a third charter added the Isles of Bermuda to the territories of the Virginia Company.

As business ventures, neither of these companies chartered in 1606 was

Indian corn and an "Indian jay" (above) appeared opposite the title page (below) of a merchant's persuasive pamphlet written in 1651 to promote the settlement of the Virginia region. The Indians had cultivated corn as their chief crop for several thousand years, considering it a legacy from their gods. Corn saved many of the lives in Jamestown in "the starving time."

THE
DISCOVERY
OF
Nevv Brittaine.
Began *August* 27. Anno Dom. 1650.

By {
 Edward Bland, Merchant.
 Abraham woode, Captaine.
 Sackford Brewster, } Gentlemen.
 Elias Peunant,
}

From Fort *Henry*, at the head of *Appamattuck* River in *Virginia*, to the Fals of *Blandina*, first River in *New Brittaine*, which runneth West; being 120. Mile South-west, between 35. & 37. degrees, (a pleasant Country,) of temperate Ayre, and fertile Soyle.

LONDON,
Printed by *Thomas Harper* for *John Stephenson*, at the Sun below Ludgate. *M.DC.LI.*

entirely satisfactory. The Plymouth Company made an unsuccessful settlement, not in northern Virginia, but on the Maine coast in New England. The efforts of the Virginia Company were more long-lasting, but their value was diminished by stockholders' battles and struggles for company control. For the first 12 years the Virginia Company was managed by Sir Thomas Smith, one of the most prominent businessmen in England. He was so preoccupied with his many enterprises that he could give very little time to the problems of settlement. Shaken by a combination of management, rising deficits and criticisms from the settlers in Virginia, he was unseated in 1619 by an opposition faction led by Sir Edwin Sandys. Sir Edwin committed the opposite mistake: he put colonizing ahead of short-term profits. His regime encouraged greatly increased emigration to Virginia and launched an overambitious program to produce a variety of staple crops. Despite these laudable efforts, the company's fortunes continued to decline. Sir Thomas Smith's group brought suit, the company was thrown into receivership, its charter was annulled in 1624, and the crown took over.

T HE early settlers in Virginia had brought with them one remarkable individual, Captain John Smith. Except for him, the leaders of the colony were all fainthearted, incompetent or mutinous. However, it is hard to separate legend from fact in the story of John Smith. Smith himself was a partisan reporter who embellished facts with wonderfully colorful details.

That Smith was a soldier of fortune, a historian and an explorer who diligently mapped the interior of the territory is generally accepted without dispute. He was also, it seems probable, at one time the slave of a Turkish pasha, in whose service he became an accomplished soldier. In addition, Smith described himself as a master of miraculous escapes and a favorite of the ladies of many nations. Both of these attributes are involved in the familiar story of Smith's encounter with Powhatan, the absolute monarch of Indian Virginia. Captured by Powhatan's men, Smith, the story goes, was about to have his brains beaten out at the chief's order. At the last moment, Pocahontas, the chief's 12-year-old daughter, rushed forward and laid her own head upon his to save him from death. Powhatan was moved by his daughter's gesture, and Smith survived to include this episode in his *Generall Historie of Virginia*, published 16 years after the event. Whether or not Smith improved the story of his deliverance, it is at least consistent with what else we know of Pocahontas. This gentle princess proved the patron saint of the Jamestown colony and brought food to the starving settlers during the critical times. In Smith's own words, "she next under God, was still the instrument to preserve this Colonie from death, famine and utter confusion."

In 1609 the Jamestown settlers who had survived the earlier hardships were reinforced by 600 new colonists. But Smith criticized the grandiose and impractical plans of the company. In place of the craftsmen they sent over to make pitch, tar, soap, ashes and glass, he entreated his superiors to let him have "but 30 Carpenters, husbandmen, gardiners, fishermen, blacksmiths, masons, and diggers up of trees, roots . . . [rather] then a thousand of such as we have." In the spring of 1609 Smith ruled that he who would not work would not eat. More important, he started the cultivation of Indian corn. Shortly afterward, the doughty captain was summarily replaced as leader of the colony by the Virginia Company. In his stead Lord Delaware served briefly as Virginia's

THE PATTERNS OF
SETTLEMENT

British colonization of the upper South was shaped by many geographic factors, principally the numerous harbors and river routes that led inland. The first tiny group of settlers in America, who were left on Roanoke Island in 1587, vanished without a trace. By 1607 the first permanent settlement, at Jamestown, was undergoing its terrible trials. One by one, Williamsburg, Richmond, St. Marys and other settlements came into existence, but in the next century and a quarter English colonizers had scarcely crept inland beyond the Tidewater lands to the Piedmont.

first governor. Even after allowance is made for Smith's vainglory, this was a shabby reward for the man who almost alone had courage, enterprise and a grasp of the problems of settling in the wilderness.

Practically all the settlers suffered from disease; Indian attacks and malnutrition took their toll; the number of colonists steadily waned until only 60 were left. To surmount the continuing crisis, Delaware's successor as governor of Virginia used dictatorial powers. Martial law was imposed and the harshest penalties were established for civilian disorder. But these measures did less for the stability of the colony than the cultivation of tobacco, the first crop that had a trading value.

In 1614, two years after colonist John Rolfe developed an effective method of curing tobacco so that it could be exported, the first crop was shipped to England. Rolfe himself went along with his bride, Pocahontas. Virginia's guardian angel and its first money crop both left marks on England. Pocahontas was a popular but ill-fated visitor. She died in England, but the memory of her popularity is still kept alive by the Cornish village, Indian Queen, that was named for her. The "sotweed," as tobacco was commonly called, had a greater impact. It had been brought to England from Virginia earlier by Sir Walter Raleigh, and no product ever achieved a more immediate and overwhelming acceptance. James I wrote a special tract against the use of tobacco, but nothing could stop the spread of the tobacco habit. As a last gesture of defiance to the king, the imperturbable Raleigh puffed a pipe of tobacco before ascending the scaffold to die in the culmination of a long series of conflicts with the crown.

It was at this point that the Virginia Company, under Sir Edwin Sandys, launched its ambitious scheme for the production of food and staples. By 1619, thanks to the tobacco crop, the promise of security and affluence for the settlement in Virginia was sufficiently clear. The company therefore felt that the colony was ready for a larger share of self-government. An assembly was convened at Jamestown in July. Consisting of the governor, his council and two representatives from each of the 11 counties, it was America's first legislative body and nothing like it had ever existed in any non-English colony. Later, the county representatives formed themselves into a second chamber, the House of Burgesses, in imitation of the Commons of England. Elated by this confirmation of their privileges as Englishmen, the settlers, a contemporary recorded, henceforward "regarded Virginia as their country," and "fell to building houses and planting corn."

Colonial newspapers abounded in notices of slave sales (below) and runaways. Escapes were so numerous that printers kept stock woodcuts (above) to which owners added the specific description. One such ad, for an 18-year-old boy, offered the finder ". . . Four Dollars reward, and all Charges paid. . . ."

P OCAHONTAS' celebrated marriage to John Rolfe had led to what was known as the "married peace" with the Indians, but these good relations ended when Powhatan died in 1618. His successor, Opechancanough, recognized the threat the English posed to the remaining lands held by the Indians, and decided to strike before the settlers became invincible by numbers alone. The attack came on the terrible morning of March 22, 1622, when the Indians surprised and massacred 347 settlers. Despite English counterattacks, Indian forays continued until the 1630s. By then there were too many Englishmen in Virginia for the Indians to take on, but in 1644 old Opechancanough again led his followers in a second massacre. Opechancanough was captured and sent to Jamestown, where he was killed by one of the settlers ordered to guard him. The Powhatan Confederacy he led was finally smashed, and farming and

hunting lands were allotted to the Indians who put themselves under the protection of the government of Virginia.

Under Governor Sir William Berkeley, the colony achieved peace. Sir William encouraged crop diversification and manufactures, and ended the poll tax. Strengthened by the arrival of numerous Royalists after the execution of Charles I in 1649, Berkeley managed to keep Anglicanism dominant despite reformist dissidents. For a time during Oliver Cromwell's rule, Berkeley was displaced by a commissioner sent by Parliament. But when the Puritan regime collapsed in 1660 and Charles II ascended the throne in the Restoration of the monarchy, Berkeley returned to power.

SIR William's second administration was much less successful. Though continuing some of his constructive policies, he became increasingly arbitrary and paternalistic. Between 1661 and 1676 he called, at most, one election of the burgesses. There were other grounds for dissatisfaction with his administration. The sharp drop in tobacco prices, brought on by England's Navigation Act of 1660, pinched pocketbooks. Burdensome taxation, a succession of bad crops, and a series of servant uprisings, in protest against working conditions on the plantations, combined to generate more tension. Berkeley's greatest crisis was precipitated by a cluster of frontier incidents which the old governor, who considered himself the protector of the Indians, seemed unable or unwilling to check.

The discontented elements in Virginia gathered around Nathaniel Bacon Jr. in an affair known as Bacon's Rebellion. Bacon was a recent emigrant from the old country who, coincidentally, was a cousin by marriage of Sir William. Headstrong and haughty, Bacon had, according to rumor, run through a fortune before he was 30. In 1676 he and others directed an unauthorized retaliatory raid against the Indians. For this highhanded action, Bacon was declared a traitor by Berkeley, but when he acknowledged his offense the governor pardoned him. "God forgive you, I forgive you," said Berkeley magnanimously. But the peace between the two rivals did not last. The same year, Bacon overthrew the colonial government. He marched his supporters into Jamestown without a fight and took over the House of Burgesses. With guns pointed at their heads, the burgesses yielded power to him, and Berkeley fled to loyal Accomac County on the Eastern Shore of Chesapeake Bay. The revolt was based on a wide range of issues: among them were demands for better frontier security, tax reforms and improved administration, and a more equitable distribution of patronage.

According to one of Bacon's intimates, a brazen liar named John Goode, he intended to have Virginia secede from the empire in the hopes that Maryland and South Carolina would join in this movement for independence. Bacon died suddenly of dysentery in October 1676, and the revolt was soon over. Bacon may have hoped only to correct certain specific grievances, or he may indeed have been a forerunner of the American Revolution. In any case, the revolt brought into the open the resentments of the servants and working-class settlers of the province.

Back in power, old Governor Berkeley hanged 23 of the rebel leaders. For this he was relieved of his office and recalled to England. Charles II, who had ascended the throne after a much more serious rebellion during which his father was beheaded, thought Berkeley's retribution was excessive. "That old

Bacon's Rebellion of 1676 featured a hot clash (above) in Jamestown. Nathaniel Bacon (right), leading 500 farmers, was met by their antagonist, Governor Berkeley, who cried, "Here, shoot me. . . ." Reformer Bacon demanded "a commission against the Heathen who daily inhumanly murder us. . . ."

fool," said the king, "has killed more people in that naked country than I have done for the murder of my father."

If the settlement of Virginia presaged the world to come with its emphasis on profits for stockholders, the establishment of the neighboring colony of Maryland reflected the world that was, in which the ownership of land was the best hallmark of quality and prestige. Ambitious Englishmen like Sir George Calvert, the first Lord Baltimore, saw in the vast spaces of America a fresh opportunity to carve out great landed estates on the English model. Lord Baltimore was also a convert to Catholicism, and he had in mind offering refuge to English Roman Catholics, whose lives were clouded by the discriminatory laws against them. To this end he helped his son Cecilius secure a grant in 1632 of an area on the upper reaches of the Chesapeake, which was named Maryland in honor of the queen, Henrietta Maria.

Among the passengers aboard the *Ark* and the *Dove* on the first voyage to Maryland in 1633, the majority were Protestant craftsmen, laborers and servants. Catholic gentlemen-adventurers were the minority, a strong indication that anti-Catholic laws were enforced only indifferently in England by Charles I, whose wife was Catholic. While the early Stuarts were hardly friendly to religious liberty, Puritans rather than Catholics were the targets of official animosity. Moreover, Lord Baltimore himself, jealous of sharing authority with anyone, ordered that the Jesuit mission to Maryland could not acquire land.

The crown charter for Maryland established a feudal seigniory with extensive powers modeled on those of the bishop of the Palatinate of Durham, a northern English county. In Durham during the Middle Ages, the bishop was allowed to exercise a quasi-regal authority in order to maintain peace on the frontier. Similarly, the absentee proprietor of Maryland, Cecilius Calvert, second Lord Baltimore, owned all the land, received all the profits from it, and had power to appoint all the officials of the colony and to dismiss them at his pleasure. However, the charter also provided that such laws as he enacted must be passed "with the Advice, Assent and Approbation of the Free-Men of the . . . Province." The freemen's views were reflected in the popular assembly, originally composed of all the citizens of the first settlement, St. Marys, near the southernmost point of Maryland's western shore. Later, when the practice of collecting proxies was introduced (much as directors of modern corporations solicit proxy votes from stockholders), the assembly lost its independence. By 1641, Calvert's officials had enough proxies to control the assembly for the entire session. But growth of the colony forced a change in 1650 to a representative legislature similar to Virginia's House of Burgesses.

MARYLAND suffered from the downward turn of affairs for the Stuart dynasty in England. Lord Baltimore lost his colony for several years, but the Restoration put things right for him, and he appointed his son Charles as governor in 1661. At his father's orders, Charles selected his council from the colonial elite: no member was lower in rank than lord of the manor. For years to come, the government of Maryland was really a family affair.

Benefiting by Virginia's experiments with tobacco, Maryland had cultivated that crop from the beginning, although European wheat and Indian corn were also grown. The long decline of tobacco prices which set in after 1660 caused serious distress. The colony also had to endure continuing disputes over proprietary rents and nepotism, and religious animosity smoldered

The first seal of the Carolinas was adopted by the eight Lords Proprietors after Charles II had granted them the territory "west, in a direct line, as far as the south seas. . . ." Presumably, the Indians on the shield are bringing tribute, although the chief's firm grip on his spear suggests the contrary.

The coins struck by Cecilius, Lord Baltimore, not only served as legal tender throughout Maryland, but underlined his proprietary authority as well. The shilling of silver (above), of 1659, bears the family arms with the motto "Increase and Multiply" on one side and a bust of Cecilius on the other side.

between Puritan and Catholic. As early as 1649, the assembly had passed an Act of Toleration granting religious freedom to all persons who believed in Christianity. A conservative piece of legislation, designed to protect the Catholic minority, the act was nonetheless a milestone in the history of religious freedom. An insurgent Puritan assembly amended it in 1654, but its provisions of toleration were reaffirmed in 1657.

Antiproprietary sentiment reached its height during the long absence of the third Lord Baltimore. He returned to England in 1684 to argue a boundary dispute with William Penn as well as to answer charges that he had favored Catholics and prevented royal customs men from doing their work. His nephew George Talbot was acting governor until he fled from the colony to avoid trial for murdering a customs official.

After the accession of William and Mary to the English throne in 1689, an insurgent band marched on the capital at St. Marys, secured its surrender and summoned the assembly. The assembly thereupon asked William and Mary to take over the province. Baltimore was allowed to keep only his property rights. The Church of England was established and the capital moved from Catholic St. Marys to Protestant Anne Arundel, now called Annapolis.

The religious conflict within Maryland lessened with the passage of time. The fourth Lord Baltimore became a convert to the Church of England and reared his children in the new faith. With this, doubts as to the family's loyalty faded and Charles, fifth Lord Baltimore, was restored in 1715 to the proprietorship, which the Baltimore family held until the American Revolution.

ALL through the 17th Century, England's definition of its American sphere of interest expanded. Elizabethan and Stuart statesmen insisted that the nation's security demanded seizure of certain key Caribbean isles. These would provide naval bases, safeguard England's sea lanes of trade (while taking them into the heart of the Spanish Empire) and protect an Atlantic domain stretching from Newfoundland to Florida. Oliver Cromwell's imperialistic designs, and his effort to police the shipping and trade of the empire for the advantage of the mother country, were expanded by the Restoration. Cromwell had planned to occupy territory south of Virginia to serve as a buffer against the ancient enemy in Spanish Florida. Under Charles II, this plan was coupled with a renewed commercial rivalry with the Dutch which culminated in the conquest of New Netherland by the English in 1664.

To a group of eight of his staunchest supporters, the king granted the vast domain of "Carolana." Included in the group were Sir John Colleton, a Royalist soldier back from exile as a planter in Barbados; Sir William Berkeley, with his vast experience as governor of Virginia; and George Monck, Duke of Albemarle, a Cromwellian general who changed sides in time and shrewdly engineered the Stuart restoration. The most prestigious member of the group was the king's companion-in-exile and first minister, Edward Hyde, the Earl of Clarendon. The real leader was Sir Anthony Ashley Cooper, better known to history as the first Earl of Shaftesbury. By the terms of the charter of 1663, this select coterie received title to roughly all the land between Florida and Virginia, westward to the "South Sea," as the Pacific was then called. Two years later the grant was extended into Florida.

Over this tremendous area the proprietors were granted absolute rule, subject only to the reservations that the laws of the province be enacted with the

THE BUILDING
OF SOUTHERN COLONIES

Many a colony in the deep coastal South started as a strategic buffer state. The Spaniards, for example, built St. Augustine to guard against French Huguenots at Fort Caroline, who were among the very earliest settlers; 170 years later the British threw up battlements of ground sea shells at Fort Frederica to watch the Spaniards. Other settlements were more prosaic. Kilted Highlanders settled New Inverness, now called Darien, and English developers established other Tidewater communities. The inland towns came later as the upland country grew more populous.

assent of the freemen or their deputies and that such laws be "agreeable to the laws and customs of England."

Perhaps the most extraordinary feature of the Carolina government was the odd mixture of feudal, monarchical and liberal ideas in an instrument of government called the Fundamental Constitutions of Carolina of 1669. The blend is believed to have been the joint product of Sir Anthony Ashley Cooper and his secretary, the renowned philosopher John Locke. Locke is best remembered today for his assertion that the state is based on a "social contract" between the people and their government. The Fundamental Constitutions aimed for a balanced government, "agreeable to the Monarchy under which we live," and free from the dangers of "a numerous democracy."

At the heart of the document was its insistence that "all power and dominion is most naturally founded on property," a notion given concrete form in the elaborate hierarchy of nobility envisaged for the colony. Nothing faintly similar to this scheme was ever again proposed in America. At the apex of Carolina society were to be the eight Lords Proprietors. Each lord was to have a seigniory of 12,000 acres in each county. Highest of the liege men were the landgraves (a term borrowed from the German peerage), holding four baronies apiece, or 48,000 acres in all. Next were the caciques (Spanish for Indian chief), each holding two baronies. Beneath this upper crust were the 3,000- to 12,000-acre lords of the manor, and lowest on the ladder were the freeholders, who could vote if they held 50 acres.

Theoretically, this economy would be sustained by the "leet-men," an old English term revived to describe settlers similar in status to villeins, the peasants of medieval England. But no leet-men ever came to the Carolinas. Slavery, accepted by the Fundamental Constitutions, provided the labor needed on plantations almost from the start.

The province was governed by the Lords Proprietors, who sat in England as the Palatine Court (so called after the palace courts of feudal nobility), a resident governor (who had to be at least a landgrave), and an assembly composed of the governor, nobility, and a freeholder holding at least 500 acres from each precinct. The freeholders ultimately sat in a lower house separate from the upper chamber of the large landowners. Strange as these provisions may seem, the fact is that at least 26 landgraves and 13 caciques were created. But no seigniory or barony ever ran to more than 12,000 acres, no manorial jurisdiction was ever exercised and most of the titles died with the original owner.

Along with a plan for social structure completely unsuited to colonial life, there were some remarkably forward-looking provisions in the Fundamental Constitutions. One provided freedom of religion: "noe person whatever shall disturbe, molest or persecute another for his Speculative opinions in Religion or his way of Worship"; however, by another provision the Church of England was given an established status.

T HE Carolinas achieved neither political nor economic unity, and soon began to split apart. The scattered northern settlements around Albemarle Sound were isolated from Virginia by the Dismal Swamp, and cut off from southern Carolina by other swamps and wilderness. The Charleston (called "Charles Town" until 1783) settlement, on the other hand, located at the junction of the Ashley and Cooper Rivers, could exploit the fertile lands which lay upriver and the Indian trade which lay beyond the headwaters. From its

KING GEORGE I

George I came from Hanover to rule England from 1714 to 1727. He was not popular. His preference for Hanover and his failure to learn English offended subjects of every class, at home and in the colonies. But because he seldom interfered, their constitutional liberties were strengthened in his reign.

KING GEORGE II

Easily bullied, George II ascended the throne (1727-1760) to be ruled by his wife and, later, his ministers. Although he railed at "that d—d house of commons," his major passions were not the affairs of state but money, music, martial displays and sophisticated women. Georgia was named for him.

magnificently located harbor, Charleston could trade with the whole world.

Early Carolina had two serious deficiencies. It had no staple crop, and it had no natural line of security against the Indians and England's national rivals, Spain to the south and France to the west. The first problem was successfully solved within two decades after settlement, when planters near Charleston learned to raise rice. By the 1690s, seed imported from Madagascar made Carolina rice the great, profitable export crop of the southern colony. The climate of the northern colony proved as inhospitable to the rice crop as to the plantation system on which cultivation was based. So the settlers in northern Carolina turned to tobacco, corn and cattle.

BY the beginning of the 18th Century, it was evident that there were two Carolinas: an aristocratic, slave-owning and affluent plantation society in the south; a rowdy, democratic and dissenting society in the north. Geography, religion, economics and society all conspired to keep the two regions apart as proprietary authority steadily dwindled.

When it became clear that the Lords Proprietors of the Carolinas could not guarantee their borders against the incursions of Spaniards, the French or the Indians, the crown had to assume responsibility. The Yamassee border wars of 1715-1728 had shown that the Spaniards were once more on the march on the southern frontier. To counter this move, the home government decided to establish the buffer settlement of Georgia.

The character of this new colony differed greatly from that of either of the Carolinas. Georgia was dominated from the beginning by two outstanding humanitarians: John Lord Viscount Percival, afterward the first Earl of Egmont, and James Edward Oglethorpe, a member of Parliament, a onetime soldier of fortune and supporter of the Stuart cause. Despite his Tory background and his impetuous youth, Oglethorpe turned into an exceptionally liberal-minded statesman who as he grew older was also at home in Dr. Samuel Johnson's intimate literary circle. Alexander Pope put him into a couplet that made reference both to his humanity and his wide journeying:

> One driven by strong benevolence of soul,
> Shall fly like Oglethorpe from pole to pole.

Both Percival and Oglethorpe had served on the committee of Parliament that investigated the plight of debtors, who were often sentenced to rot in festering prisons. One outgrowth of this investigation was the passage of legislation setting free several categories of debtors. The founders of Georgia hoped that their colony could salvage the imprisoned debtor and offer him a life of usefulness. They also considered their colony as a possible haven for Protestants persecuted by Catholic monarchs in Europe.

Thus there were two objectives that shaped the charter which the crown granted for Georgia in 1732. One was the need for border stability. The other was the fulfillment of the founders' idealistic goals. That portion of the old Carolina grant lying between the Altamaha and the Savannah Rivers and extending from sea to sea was turned over to a group of trustees for 21 years, after which the colony would revert to the crown. The trustees were forbidden to derive personal profit either from officeholding or from the appropriation of land. All government was vested in the Trustees' Council in London and no provision made for self-rule. Supported by private benevolence, the colony did

Colonel James Edward Oglethorpe, "the beau-ideal of an English gentleman," spent his fortune and ran into debt trying to create an ideal society in Georgia. For his pains he was summoned home and court-martialed in 1743. The charges, lodged by his jealous aide, proved "malicious and groundless," and in a tardy gesture he was promoted to general 22 years later.

not have to impose taxes, and therefore had no need for a representative assembly to levy taxes. Since Georgia was planned as a paternalistic settlement for unfortunate settlers, there seemed no reason to allot them any responsibility for their own welfare.

The trustees' regulations limited family holdings to 50 acres with a view to re-establishing the fast-vanishing yeoman class of England. All grants were inalienable and descended by entail to eldest sons; they could not be lost through improvidence. Other laws forbade the importation of rum and brandy and banned the introduction of slavery. Oglethorpe treated the Creek Indians fairly; he even purchased from them the land needed for settlement. He was a benefactor to the Moravians, a small Protestant sect from central Europe, and a loyal friend to the Jewish colonists when some settlers sought to expel them. Hospitality was extended to German Lutherans, Scotch Highlanders, to the Methodist leader John Wesley and his magnetic colleague, George Whitefield. However, only a small number of imprisoned debtors decided to seek asylum in Georgia; and some of these backslid and went into debt almost immediately upon arrival. Considering the auspices under which the colony was founded, it is rather sad to note that most of the permanent settlers were small-minded conformists. Lacking the generosity and tolerance of an Oglethorpe, they wanted nothing better than to live like rich Carolina planters—off the labor of African slaves.

One by one, the Georgia colonists chipped away at the restrictions on their right to accumulate, to spend and to exploit others. One after another, the cherished ideals which animated the trust were compromised. By the time a disillusioned set of trustees turned the colony over to administration by the crown, Georgia was just another British rice-planting colony, the southernmost link in the slender chain of settlements that constituted the British Empire in North America.

John Wesley, the founder of Methodism, came as a missionary to preach in the "Georgian Utopia." He stayed only two years, until 1738. It was long enough for him to woo a pretty parishioner, to be sued for defamation of character and to stir up considerable ill will with his rigid ecclesiastical methods (from which was derived the name of his evangelical faith).

DESPITE variations in population, economic interests and geographic conditions, the southern colonies conformed to a pattern more closely resembling that which prevailed in the British West Indian islands than that which might be found in the northern settlements. All the southern colonies were examples of that mixed enterprise by which England colonized North America. The thrust to settlement was provided by the crown in the form of generous land grants, but the management and control in all cases were initially in the hands of private companies or proprietors, and in the case of Georgia, of trustees. Save for Maryland, however, all were destined to become crown colonies. While public benevolence played some role in the founding of the southern colonies, the pulse of religion did not pound with the same loud beat as in New England nor did the southern clergy ever acquire the prestige or power that they quickly won in the Puritan colonies of the North.

Taken by themselves, these characteristics might not have created an unbridgeable gap between the northern and southern colonies. But there was more. Land tenure in the South was marked by the accumulation of many large estates. This, in turn, gave rise to a yawning abyss between the very rich and the very poor. Moreover, the spread of slavery made this a society whose continuance depended on a rigid discipline. These two features were to give to southern life a distinctiveness and a sense of separatism, creating, in the course of time, a nation within a nation.

Land systems in the colonial South

IN 1622, fifteen years after Jamestown was founded, colonizing in Virginia remained so perilous that the settlement was almost wiped out in a single day *(below)*. But emigrants kept coming to the southern Tidewater: here were small farms for the landless, huge estates to signal the gentry's wealth and social standing. How this immense forest domain was distributed and put to use imposed on the South patterns that still affect it deeply.

In all of the southern colonies, it took about a century for similar conditions to produce the same land system. Through the early decades, the enormous problems of establishing a community so far from home exhausted the colonies' money and manpower, leaving them hard put to survive. In the middle decades, individual enterprise replaced group efforts and objectives, and each colony expanded as its residents, steadily increasing, competed vigorously for unoccupied land. But farming was expensive even after the land had been cleared: the cost of labor and of shipping crops to market in England remained high. In the more stable later decades, as the supply of slaves began to meet the need for labor, the lower costs of farming large holdings made them effective monopolies. By the outbreak of the Revolution, the plantation system had become the social as well as the economic framework of the South.

Indians massacre the settlers on a Jamestown plantation in 1622. One day's raids claimed 347 lives.

A STANCH COLONIZER, Sir Walter Raleigh is considere by some Virginia's first hero. He sent five parties to th region, whose name honors Elizabeth, the "Virgin Queen.

Captain John Smith

Pocahontas in England

The steady rise to power of large Virginia planters

WHEN Jamestown was founded, investors in the parent Virginia Company were entitled to 100 acres for each share of stock they owned. But the colony's early experiments as a classless and communal society proved to be a complete fiasco. The gentlemen-adventurers showed little interest in farming the land; those who had come to work were quickly discouraged by long, hard labor, without pay, on publicly owned fields; and few colonists were able to make full use of their holdings. In spite of the strong rule of Captain John Smith and the constant help of Pocahontas, scarcely 1,200 settlers—about a quarter of all the arrivals of 17 years—survived to see the company charter revoked in 1624.

But in the next 50 years, Jamestown made remarkable progress. Then the key colonists were diligent small farmers. Their neat freeholds, 50 to 500 acres put mostly to tobacco, pushed back the forest and spread upstream along the James River. But the very success of the small farmers helped prove their undoing, for it attracted entrepreneurs with matchless resources—cash, political influence and social connections. These large operators easily obtained big land grants and expanded them by shrewd management. The small farmers of the frontier, unable to compete with the Tidewater plantations and left unprotected from Indian attack, made a vain protest against their lot during Bacon's Rebellion of 1676. Afterward, even though the vast majority of farms continued to average about 200 acres, great personal holdings of thousands of acres dominated the economy of Virginia.

DASHING EXPLOITS of Captain John Smith are illustrated with engravings from Smith's enormously popular *Generall Historie of Virginia, New-England, and the Summer Isles,* published in

1624. In two panels, at lower left and upper right, Smith is seen capturing Indian chiefs, and at lower right his life is saved by Pocahontas, the daughter of Chief Powhatan. Smith has often been judged a braggart and a liar, but his maps, such as the one of Virginia above, were accurate, and recent scholarship substantiates some of his unlikeliest tales of adventure.

Impractical schemes in a regimented utopia

IN SAVANNAH, barracks-like houses are erected on streets laid out with military precision. This view, made in 1734, shows James Oglethorpe's tent under the tall pines along the river.

IN 1732, when Georgia's trustees sent James Oglethorpe to build Savannah *(left)*, their ample funds and high ideals promised that the colony would be a unique success. However, the trustees alienated the poor settlers whom they wanted to help by saddling them with severe restrictions; and their well-intentioned decrees against slave labor and large-scale farms banned the very means by which the other southern colonies had developed.

Typical of their experimental and repressive measures was a decree that two mulberry trees per acre must be planted on all land grants—as food for silkworms. At first, silk-producing showed promise: Oglethorpe took eight pounds of raw silk to London in 1734; two years later the trustees proudly announced that Georgia silk had been woven into a gown for Queen Caroline. But the trustees' restrictions discouraged further immigration and investment. Many skilled German silk workers, who had arrived as refugees *(below)*, moved away in disgust. Hard experience finally forced the scrapping of most of Georgia's impractical regulations and projects. Silk production dwindled after the subsidies that had fostered it were withdrawn; and by the time of the Revolution, little remained of the local industry but plantations with names like Wormsloe, Mulberry Grove and Silk Hope.

TYROLEAN LUTHERANS, persecuted in Catholic Salzburg (in what is now Austria), begin their long trek to Georgia. By 1741, about 1,200 German-speaking refugees had come to the colony.

VISITING LONDON in 1734, James Oglethorpe, dressed in black *(opposite)*, presents to his colony's trustees a group of Indians who sold him land and pledged amity the year before.

This peaceful settlement is Baltimore as it looked in 1752—a village of 100 people, 25 houses, two inns and a church. Cash crops like

Manorial farms and tenantry in Maryland

CECILIUS CALVERT, second Lord Baltimore, is seen with his grandson. A Catholic, he envisioned Maryland, granted to his father in 1632, as a haven for refugees of all faiths.

PRESTIGE and religious freedom as well as profit induced the second Lord Baltimore *(left)*, Catholic proprietor of the province of Maryland, to send settlers there in 1633 and grant no fewer than 60 feudal manors averaging 3,000 acres. But over the years, great landholders could not afford the luxury of unproductive forests or the uneconomic practice of small-scale farming. With manpower chronically in short supply, the competition grew fierce for workers to farm small sections on lease. In the 18th Century, wealthy owners like Charles Carroll spent huge sums recruiting tenant farmers in Europe and the northern colonies, paying their passage and cost of housing. As immigration swelled the ranks of tenants, Carroll was able, through skilled overseers, to develop several large and lucrative plantations; and land that produced no income in 1734 was yielding more than 50,000 pounds of tobacco per annum 30 years later.

tobacco, growing at right, promoted intensive farming, which scattered the population and retarded the growth of towns in the South.

COLONIAL SPORTSMEN bred to the saddle ride on a fox hunt, popular in Virginia and Maryland by the middle 1700s. Little used as draft animals in the early years, horses ran wild and were hunted with dog packs. In the 18th Century, blooded stallions for breeding were being imported from England, and a racing stable became the crowning touch on a gentleman's estate.

CAROLINIAN Arthur Middleton, inheritor of great estates from both parents, is shown with his wife and son in a warm portrait *(right)* by Benjamin West. A signer of the Declaration of Independence, Middleton owned more than 50,000 acres and 800 slaves.

SLAVE CABINS stand in rows *(left)* behind Mulberry Castle, a fortresslike mansion in which women and children could take refuge during Indian attack. By 1715, the colony's slaves, Indians as well as blacks, far outnumbered some 6,000 white residents.

A GAY PARTY of officers and gentlemen *(right)* spends an evening at one of the numerous plantations of the distinguished Manigault family. In the cartoon, drawn by a guest (at foot of table, lower left), Peter Manigault (to his left) says, "Your toast, Howarth."

The first metropolis in a plantation empire

AROUND Charleston, land was valued at a penny an acre late in the 17th Century. Thus a would-be planter did not require a princely purse to join Carolina's quaint and artificial peerage, becoming a cacique with 24,000 acres, or even a landgrave with 48,000 acres. But for several decades, because of the persistent shortage of labor and the heavy cost of starting large-scale operations, most of these tracts were only partially cultivated, and at little profit.

A direct result was the sale and subdivision of many vast holdings. In one typical chain of transactions, Sir Anthony Ashley Cooper, one of the colony's Lords Proprietors, sold a barony of 12,000 acres to merchant Samuel Wragg in 1712. Three years later, Wragg sold half of this land to Alexander Skene and Jacob Satur. In 1716, Satur resold his 3,000-acre portion, which was presently broken down and sold off in many small parcels.

But land was not the only route to membership in the aristocracy. Some Carolinians invested in the fur trade, the slave trade, the rich traffic with the West Indies, the promising start of intercolony commerce. One of the smaller planters, Pierre Manigault, a French Huguenot who had arrived in Carolina around 1695, was quick to capitalize on the lively town economy that was making Charleston the first city of the colonial South. Moving in from the country, he parlayed the revenue from an inn into a brandy distillery, a cooperage and a mercantile firm. After his death in 1729, his son Gabriel expanded the trading business, married into a well-connected family and invested in a number of plantations. By the 1750s Gabriel had become one of the wealthiest men in the province; his son Peter, Speaker of South Carolina's Commons House of Assembly, was enjoying the leisured life (below) that characterized the colony's aristocracy.

A self-contained community

In the early 1700s, after long and slow development, the plantation system began to raise up in the South its ultimate product—splendid colonial mansions like Carter's Grove (above), which still stands overlooking the James River near Williamsburg, Virginia. Begun by Robert "King" Carter, whose holdings

included 300,000 acres and 1,000 slaves, this "great house" was completed around 1750 by his grandson Carter Burwell. As William Byrd II said of his nearby estate of Westover, Carter's Grove existed "in a Kind of Independence [of] every one but Providence." It grew its own food, had its own stables, craft shops and labor force; and from private docks its main crop, tobacco, was shipped directly to London. Under the powerful influence of such plantations, the South developed as a succession of provincial backwaters, largely out of touch with each other until the Revolution involved them in a common cause.

4. THE NORTHERN COLONIES

IN as eloquent a passage as is found in any account of the American adventure, William Bradford, chronicler of the *Mayflower's* passengers' early years in America, tells how the weary emigrants, finally making safe harbor on the desolate shore of Cape Cod, "fell upon their knees & blessed ye God of heaven, who had brought them over ye vast & furious ocean." It was November, "and ye whole countrie, full of woods and thickets, represented a wild and savage heiw." Behind the voyagers was a mighty ocean, and there was little hope of succor from their friends abroad. Now nothing could sustain them but "the Spirit of God and His Grace."

It is still a matter for wonder that the little group should have made so perilous a journey. True, there were economic pressures on its members, as there were on other Englishmen who founded the northern colonies that stretched from Maine to Pennsylvania. But the Puritan leadership also was moved by an apocalyptic vision of a New Zion where their people could worship God in their own way. In a sermon preached in 1630 aboard the ship *Arbella*, bound from Southampton to Boston with Puritan emigrants, John Winthrop, founder of the Massachusetts Bay settlement, reminded his hearers that "the God of Israel is among us. . . . He shall make us a praise and glory, that men shall say of succeeding plantations: 'The Lord make it like that of New England.'"

Bradford, Winthrop and other men of intense religious conviction were representative of the considerable number of 17th Century Englishmen unwilling

FRIENDSHIP WITH THE INDIANS, key to Pennsylvania's prosperity, is confirmed by William Penn in a meeting in 1682. The painting is owned by Gilcrease Institute of Tulsa.

to accept the Church of England's compromise position between Roman Catholicism and Protestantism. These discontented people were called "Puritans" because they wanted to purify the Church of England, scrap the prayer book in favor of the Bible, simplify the ritual and observe the Sabbath strictly. Agreed on the goal, the Puritans were divided on the means. Many of them wanted a national church like the Presbyterian Church of Scotland or John Calvin's theocracy established in 1541 in Geneva. In place of archbishops and bishops they proposed a central church government, buttressed by the presbytery (ministers and lay elders) of the parish churches.

Other Puritans, called Congregationalists, wanted completely self-governing churches, each church formed by a solemn covenant entered into by the "visible saints" (those who confessed their faith and swore to the covenant). Since the Congregationalists let each congregation choose its own pastor and officers, the Presbyterians denounced them as "democratical," then a term of severe reproach. Congregationalists were not really democratic, for they admitted only the "saints" to full church fellowship, never the unregenerate rank and file. But both Presbyterians and Congregationalists hoped to remain within the Church of England and win control of it in order to achieve their purifying reforms. The Congregationalist Puritans made up the bulk of the settlers in the Massachusetts Bay Colony, which centered on Boston, and they differentiated themselves from the more extreme Separatist Puritans, popularly known as Pilgrims, who were the first Puritan group to settle in Massachusetts. (The name "Pilgrims," though it appears in William Bradford's history, *Of Plymouth Plantation*, was not generally used by the Pilgrims to describe themselves; it only came into popular usage in the 1840s in the wake of a wave of antiquarian enthusiasm for the settlers of Plymouth.)

The Pilgrims had made a clean break with the Anglican Church nearly a generation before their epochal voyage and settlement at Plymouth. The Bay Colony Puritans, on the other hand, professed themselves members of the Church of England who defended their right to criticize the established religion. The difference between the two Puritan groups, however, was more of tone than substance; once in America, the Puritans, like the Pilgrims, set up a separate church. The Pilgrims, as the more openly radical religious group, had been among the first to face persecution by King James I, and were forced to flee to Holland in 1607 and 1608. Their years in the medieval university town of Leyden, although free from persecution, were far from satisfactory. The Pilgrims found it hard to make a living in Leyden, they were not happy to see their children growing up in a foreign land, and they feared that if Spain reconquered Holland it would mean the terrors of the Inquisition for them.

D ESPITE all this, only a minority of the Leyden congregation chose to emigrate to America. These somehow raised money in London to buy a leaky ship, the 60-ton *Speedwell*. But this had to be abandoned in England, and the passengers crowded on to a larger, three-masted companion ship named the *Mayflower*. When they finally set sail on September 16, 1620, the Pilgrim men, women and children, who called themselves "Saints," numbered 51 of the 101 passengers on board; there were 50 non-Pilgrim "Strangers," including "goodmen" (ordinary settlers), hired hands and indentured servants.

The Pilgrims had arranged for passage to lands controlled by the Virginia Company. But the *Mayflower* did not head for Virginia, probably because of

Resolute Governor John Winthrop firmly guided Massachusetts in its early years. But before he died in 1649 he was saddened by what he viewed as his colony's moral decline. "This Land," he lamented, "growes weary of her Inhabitants. . . . Men . . . suffer all ruffianlike . . . disorder to passe uncontrolled."

Born in Massachusetts only three years after Harvard College was founded in 1636, Increase Mather served his alma mater as president for 16 of his 84 years. His 130 books and pamphlets and his countless sermons enunciated the rigorous standard of Puritan behavior for longer than six decades.

warnings that the Pilgrims would be inhospitably received. The decision to change the ship's course so angered the "Strangers" that a mutiny seemed imminent when the *Mayflower* anchored off what is now Provincetown on Cape Cod. With an amazing demonstration of leadership, the small group of adult male "Saints" persuaded most of the other men aboard ship, including goodmen and servants, to sign a compact by which they agreed to form themselves into "a civil body Politick" and promised "all due Submission and Obedience" to its "just and equall lawes." The Mayflower Compact was the first example of the plantation covenant, used later by the settlers in Connecticut, New Hampshire and Rhode Island. It helped establish the American tradition of government resting upon the consent of the governed. Having created their own commonwealth, the Pilgrims then elected Deacon John Carver as the first New World governor chosen by free people in a free election.

It was late in 1620 when the Pilgrims decided upon Plymouth, across Cape Cod Bay from Provincetown, for their permanent settlement. With the help of friendly neighboring Indians, the survivors of the first dreadful winter slowly built their settlement. After an early experiment with communal planting, the Pilgrims relied instead on individual farming, with better results.

But the little colony lacked the essentials for growth. Its leadership was largely uneducated and Plymouth was culturally backward. Its farm land was not good and the colony was poorly located for the fur trade and fishing. So it remained small, and in 1691 New England's first permanent settlement was finally taken over by the increasingly powerful Massachusetts Bay Colony.

In contrast to the Pilgrims, the Puritan settlers of the Bay Colony, who did not arrive in America until 1630, quickly founded a dozen or more towns and induced many thousands to come to New England within the decade following their arrival. The group of Puritan leaders who set up the Massachusetts Bay Company received a charter in 1629 which granted stockholders or freemen authority to govern the colony. But by accident or design (the colony's first governor, John Winthrop, called it deliberate), the charter had no provision requiring that company headquarters be in England, as was usual with English corporations. Therefore it was possible to transfer the company, the charter and the whole government to New England. This corporate structure was slowly changed into a virtually sovereign commonwealth; first through increasing the number of freeholders, later by substituting a representative legislature for the meeting of stockholders.

John Winthrop, the lawyer who led this Puritan migration, came from a family of substance, had studied at Trinity College, Cambridge, and had served as justice of the peace and lord of the manor. With a large family to support, Winthrop thought that prospects were better in the New World, and his religious conviction as a Puritan fortified his economic resolve.

When Winthrop sailed for Massachusetts in 1630, he left behind an England where economic prospects were poor. The Thirty Years' War was ravaging the Continent. England's important export trade in woolen cloth was strangled, and goods piled up at the docks. Consequently, weavers and spinners were thrown out of work. A succession of bad harvests added hunger to the nation's economic distress. Despair spread throughout the country, perhaps cutting most deeply in the counties where weaving was the principal industry and where the Puritans were most numerous. Driven by discontent,

THE RAPID EXPANSION
OF EARLY NEW ENGLAND

Still thriving cities like Boston and Providence confirm the wisdom of the early settlers in selecting locations. By 1640, energetic immigrants had established important inland centers. Eastern Long Island, by agreement with the Dutch at New Amsterdam, was likewise open to the English, and colonists from the mainland made it virtually part of New England. Long before the Pilgrims landed, the first English settlement in the area was founded at Popham Beach, where New England's first ship was built. But after a year these settlers fled Maine's harsh winter.

people reached out to other lands. During the Great Migration from 1630 to 1643, some 20,000 embarked for New England, while some 45,000 went to the southern colonies and the West Indies.

But economic hardship was only a partial explanation of the discontent. There was great antagonism to the personal rule of Charles I, and particularly to the torture and jailing of leading dissenters, which increased when William Laud became archbishop of Canterbury in 1633. Intense Puritan reformers like William Prynne were fined, imprisoned, even branded and mutilated. Puritan preachers were restrained. Many prominent ministers found it safer to take refuge in New England than to face Laud's unremitting surveillance. The émigrés included men like Thomas Hooker, the founder of Connecticut; Charles Chauncy, Harvard College's second president; John Cotton, England's leading nonconformist minister; and John Davenport, founder of New Haven Colony. Indeed, no New World colony ever began with so many theologically trained minds or college graduates as Massachusetts Bay.

Few colonies came close to Massachusetts Bay in its ability to make enemies both within and without its borders. This was almost inevitable in the light of the policies of this austere Bible commonwealth. The elders—despite their own recent persecution—emulated other rulers of the time in their abhorrence of democracy, religious toleration and separation of church and state. From the start, the Bay Colony confined voting to members of the approved Puritan churches and denied freedom of speech to its opponents.

The colony's first and most aristocratic enemy was Sir Ferdinando Gorges, who had earlier received a royal patent covering both Massachusetts and Maine, which he proposed to rule as a principality. Gorges tried to have the Puritans' charter annulled on the ground that they were acting as an independent nation and defying royal authority. But legal costs of Gorges' lawsuit ruined him, and he died before he could get the charter revoked.

OTHER enemies of the colony fared little better. The Puritans, who had suffered under the persecution of Archbishop Laud in England, now used similar tactics against opponents in Massachusetts. To Governor Winthrop, there was no excuse for liberty to think or act contrary to the covenant between God and man—as interpreted by the Puritans. The only liberty he tolerated was the liberty to do that "which is good, just and honest." "Whatsoever crosseth this," Winthrop warned, "is not authority, but a distemper thereof."

Pleasure-loving Thomas Morton of Merrymount shocked the proper Massachusetts folk with his drinking bouts, roistering and dancing around maypoles, and was twice arrested and deported. A clergyman, the learned and fearless Roger Williams was a more formidable opponent. In brilliant sermons, he infuriated the Bay Colony magistrates by denying their assertions that they exercised authority as the spiritual descendants of the prophets of Israel, and argued that the government had no sanction to punish for religious offenses. On a more mundane level, perhaps the most irritating of all his contentions was his challenge to the validity of the Bay Colony's land title, for he insisted that only the Indians, not the king, could convey land. In the dead of winter of 1636 Williams was cast out of righteous Massachusetts and forced to make his way through the trackless wilderness to Rhode Island.

Roger Williams has in recent times been praised as a founder of the American liberal tradition. In his theology a man who strained his ingenuity to find

Nonconformist Anne Hutchinson steadfastly faced her accusers in Boston, who excommunicated her and ordered her expelled "as a leper" with her husband and their 14 children. Ultimately, she settled on a river in Westchester County, near modern New York City. In 1643 she and nearly all her household were killed by Indians. The river was named in her honor.

mystical meanings in the Bible, Williams in his public actions was a notable humanitarian and social reformer. In Rhode Island he established the traditions of liberty of conscience and the separation of church and state. He favored civil rights and due process, and strongly advocated the democratic process in all aspects of life, including land distribution.

Roger Williams was the first in an honorable line of talented people lost to Massachusetts by its uncompromising Puritanism. The second was Anne Hutchinson. A woman of rare intellect, superabundant energy and great personal magnetism, she came under the spell of John Cotton when he preached in England. When Cotton fled to Massachusetts, Anne Hutchinson followed, with her husband and children. In Boston she set up a discussion center in her front parlor, where she analyzed the sermons of the town's ministers. As her following grew, she charged the Boston ministers with sticking to the letter of the Mosaic law and neglecting its spirit. She insisted that grace, the gift of the Lord's spirit, was evidenced by a serenity of soul; mere pietism and outward religious observance would not suffice.

The town of Boston was hotly pro-Hutchinson, and the conservatives, fearing defeat in the 1637 election of the governor and magistrates, transferred the meeting of the General Court, the central governing body, to a town across the river. There a rump session defeated Sir Henry Vane, favored by the Hutchinson camp. Disillusioned, he sailed for England. The Reverend John Wheelwright, Anne Hutchinson's brother-in-law and one of her chief followers, was condemned for sedition and contempt, and expelled to New Hampshire. Then Anne Hutchinson was arrested and brought to trial. Goaded beyond endurance by the court's frequent unjudicial outbursts of rancor, she declared she had learned the truth through "an immediate revelation." The court was outraged by the substitution of her own vision for the authoritative interpretation of the Bible by the ministry. She was imprisoned and then banished.

A few Presbyterian dissenters were jailed and fined in 1646 and 1647, and four Quakers who returned to Massachusetts after expulsion were executed in 1659. In 1664 a royal investigation led to a recommendation that the Massachusetts charter be revoked because the colony still denied religious liberty to non-Puritans and refused to repeal laws derogatory to the crown. But the Puritan leadership managed to delay this until 1684, when England finally abrogated the old charter.

Dissenter Roger Williams, fleeing from Salem in 1636 to avoid arrest, was met by friendly Indians who sheltered him for the winter. In his "Key," a book about Indian life and language, he helped establish the "Noble Savage" theme. Though deeply religious, Williams made few attempts at proselyting the Indians. "Forced worship," he said, "stincks in God's nostrils."

THE discontented and the rejected of Massachusetts founded new Zions of their own. Thomas Hooker felt that the people should have a greater voice in their government, and so he advocated "a general council chosen by all" instead of a legislature picked by the church members, as in the Bay Colony. These were shocking notions, even to Hooker's friend John Cotton, who felt that God never ordained democracy "as a fitt government eyther for church or Commonwealth." In their search for a place to settle, Hooker and his followers were attracted by the wide meadows of the Connecticut Valley, which offered better economic prospects than Massachusetts, where the best available land seemed already pre-empted. In 1635 Hooker led a few hundred kindred spirits from Newtown (now Cambridge) to new homes in three Connecticut "plantations" at Hartford, Wethersfield and Windsor. In 1639 these towns issued their "Fundamental Orders," a social compact by which they set up a government similar in constitutional structure to that of Massachusetts.

However, they based suffrage on property rather than a religious qualification; by 1658 the franchise was granted to those holding property worth £30 or more. But those with the requisite property qualifications had to secure the approval of the General Court. And there is some question whether the magistrates actually did accept voters who were not of the proper "religious carriage." Connecticut may have been more democratic in tone than Massachusetts, but scarcely so in fact, and a government dominated by a select Puritan coterie ruled in relative calm throughout its colonial history.

A DISCONTENT different from Hooker's spurred the Puritan scholar John Davenport and his associate Theophilus Eaton, a former London merchant, to found a strict theocracy at New Haven in 1638. Hooker and his followers thought Massachusetts' government was too strict. Davenport considered it too loose and took to New Haven John Cotton's proposed code of laws, the "Model of Moses his Judicialls," of 1636 which the Bay Colony magistrates considered too extreme. This code served as the town's fundamental law for a quarter century. But in 1662 John Winthrop Jr., long a leading man of affairs in Connecticut, persuaded Charles II to issue a charter for all of Connecticut, thus ending the little New Haven theocracy's unique system of government.

Of all the New England colonies, Rhode Island won speediest notoriety as a haven for those nonconformists who disputed the Bay Colony's brand of Puritanism. The orthodox in the Bay Colony called Rhode Island the "black sheep of the New England flock" and it was a constant target for reprisals from its neighbors. Granted a patent by Parliament in 1644, Rhode Island combined in a federal union Roger Williams' town of Providence, the communities of Portsmouth and Newport founded by Anne Hutchinson and her followers, and the village of Warwick developed by the intensely individualistic Samuel Gorton. Under Rhode Island's constitution of 1647, church membership was not a requirement for voting. Other advanced notions included initiative, referendum and recall of officers.

These and other democratic provisions reflected Williams' own democratic views, and his dedication to religious tolerance was later approved by the royal charter granted in 1663. In a letter to the town of Providence, Williams compared the colony to a ship with a mixed passenger list of Protestants, Catholics, Jews and Moslems. The ship's captain had sole command of its course and was responsible for order on the vessel, but he could not force his passengers to attend the ship's prayers. Smallest of the Thirteen Colonies, Rhode Island in time went the way of most utopias. It disfranchised Catholics in 1729, denied Jews the right of naturalization (though otherwise tolerant toward them) and turned Newport into a thriving center for the slave trade. And, contrary to the aspirations of its founder, its government fell more and more under the control of a monopolistic landowning minority.

Both centrifugal and centripetal forces were at work in 17th Century New England. The first force scattered outcasts or opponents of the Bay Colony to build settlements elsewhere. Sir Ferdinando Gorges, the Puritans' old enemy, claimed Maine under the 1629 grant from the old Council for New England, and named his cousin Thomas Gorges deputy governor of that northern outpost. Thomas Gorges' rule along Puritan lines attracted many Puritan emigrants from the Bay Colony, and the mother colony ultimately bought out the heirs of Gorges in 1691. From that time until 1820, Maine remained under the

King Philip, the Indian chief who initiated a fierce war against the New England colonies, was shown by Paul Revere, firmly gripping his musket. Actually named Metacom, the colonists gave him a royal nickname for his proud manner and his way of referring to England's Charles II as "my brother."

jurisdiction of Massachusetts. In another instance John Wheelwright, exiled during the Anne Hutchinson fracas, took refuge in 1638 at Exeter in New Hampshire, which Massachusetts soon claimed as within its charter bounds. That claim was lost in the courts, and New Hampshire was made a royal province in 1679.

Yet if differences divided them, common problems and perils forced the settlers of New England to consult with each other. Land grants were so vague that every colony had boundary arguments with its neighbor. Every colony feared Indian risings. The Dutch opposed English colonial expansion in the Connecticut Valley; the French threatened to push south from Canada. These dangers prompted the four Puritan colonies of Massachusetts Bay, Connecticut, Plymouth and New Haven to form a league in 1643, popularly called the New England Confederation. Each colony sent two commissioners to the confederation; six votes were necessary for all decisions. The confederation was directed as much against the outcast Rhode Island plantation as against the more serious menace of the Dutch and French, but during its 40-year life it also settled boundary disputes, returned runaway slaves and servants to their owners, and put down the last great wave of attacks launched by the New England Indians.

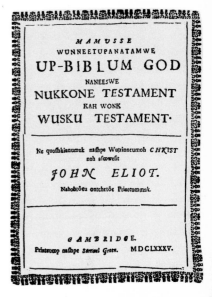

I<small>N</small> New England, and in all the English colonies, the Indian had less and less place. European technology had revolutionized Indian life. Trade goods—guns, implements, cloth—induced the tribesmen to revert from farming to hunting. Hungry for trade goods, the Indian was willing to barter furs, land and even loyalty, as a fighting ally or a benevolent neutral.

Relations between the New England colonists and the Indians had, with a few exceptions, been good from the start. After the short-lived Pequot uprising in 1637, when New England forces led by Captain John Mason destroyed the Indian stronghold on the Mystic River in Connecticut, the Indians lived at peace with the New England settlers for almost 40 years. Then King Philip, sachem of the Wampanoag, a tribe dwelling near the Plymouth settlement, realized that the growing English settlements would soon push the Indians out of the whole area. Philip held secret parleys with other related tribes and launched a number of raids against Plymouth Colony in 1675. Responding to this threat, the New England Confederation decided to crush the Indians once and for all. After three years of terrorizing raids on exposed settlements, in which the fighting spread to the upper Connecticut Valley, King Philip's allies begged for peace. Philip himself was shot, and his wife and nine-year-old son were captured and sold into slavery in the West Indies. Many towns were left in ruins; among them, Brookfield, Northfield, Deerfield, Middleborough and Warwick had been totally destroyed. The towns of Springfield, Providence, Lancaster and Groton were badly damaged, and nearly 1,000 white settlers lost their lives. From this time on, the danger from the tribesmen of New England was over, save for Indians on the Maine frontier who would from time to time join with the French in border raids on the English colonists.

The Indian-language Bible (above) and the "New-England Primer" (below) were two of the first books printed in America. Eliot's translation appeared in 1663. The primer, printed in Boston in 1690, was the only grade school textbook in the New England colonies for 50 years, and was used for 150 years.

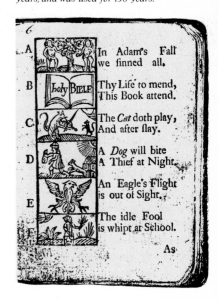

To conservative Puritan leaders like Increase Mather, the Indian Wars were God's punishment for the visible dwindling of religious observance and for such "provoking evils" as "the younger and meaner sorte" of colonist living and dressing in an ostentatious manner. Also to Mather, the threat of

Jacob Leisler, who rebelled against strict colonial rule in New York City in 1689, lived in this substantial but simple house in what is now Manhattan's financial district. The Dutch influence in architecture, seen in this roof with stepped gables, was still prevalent in mid-18th Century New York.

Divine retribution was implicit in other events. In 1688, after the enemies of the Bay Colony had succeeded in having the charter revoked, Sir Edmund Andros, the new royal governor, incorporated Massachusetts into a Dominion of New England, comprising all the plantations of that region, along with New York and the Jerseys. Andros insisted on religious toleration for Anglicans, re-examined land titles, levied taxes on his own initiative and curtailed local government. All these acts posed an enormous threat to the Puritan oligarchy. When news arrived in Boston in 1688 of England's Glorious Revolution, which ended absolute monarchy and established Parliamentary supremacy, it became the signal for an armed uprising by the colonists. Andros, as an appointee of the deposed James II, was overthrown. Increase Mather, who had previously slipped away to England, returned in 1691 with a new royal charter for Massachusetts which confirmed the powers of the oligarchy in the Bay Colony. However, Connecticut and Rhode Island kept their original charters and operated under them until the Revolution.

In setting up its Atlantic colonies, the government of England followed no systematic blueprint. As a result, its 17th Century settlements, mostly privately sponsored, were widely scattered. England's great commercial rivals, the Dutch, seized on one of the gaps and entrenched themselves in the rich and inviting area between the New England colonies and the tobacco provinces. Ironically, the Dutch penetration was initiated by a persevering and imaginative English navigator, Henry Hudson. Hired by the Dutch East India Company to search for a Northwest Passage to the wealth of Asia, Hudson sailed the *Half Moon* into New York harbor in 1609, and then proceeded up the majestic river that bears his name. When he neared what is now Albany, he realized that he had not found a water route to the Orient. But his enthusiastic reports on the fertility of the great valley and the possibilities of profitable fur trading brought Dutch traders to the scene within a few years.

In 1621 the Dutch government gave the Dutch West India Company a charter to trade and colonize. This private business enterprise chose the governor

This view of New Amsterdam, the earliest known, was published in 1651, twenty-seven years after the Dutch first settled and built their fort on lower Manhattan Island. The windmill ground grain, cultivated on the island's rich farms or brought by Indians who traveled around the island by canoe.

or director-general, and prescribed the rules of government. In 1624 some 30 families were permanently settled in the colony, and two years later, in a famous transaction, Peter Minuit, the director-general, purchased Manhattan from Canarsie Indian chiefs for trinkets worth 60 guilders (often termed equivalent to 24 gold dollars) and named the settlement New Amsterdam.

The Dutch effort to enlarge this settlement failed for three important reasons. Their land policy was shortsighted in its neglect of the small freeholder, their leadership was inept and their arbitrary company rule contrasted unfavorably with the self-government of neighboring English colonies. Under a Charter of Freedoms and Exemptions, it granted enormous manorial estates fronting 16 miles along navigable rivers and extending inland as far as settlement would permit. To qualify, the patroon (as the grantee was called) had to promise to bring 50 settlers to New Netherland. In return, the patroons got feudal rights, including exemption from taxation for eight years. Of the five patroonships set up by 1630, the only one firmly established was Rensselaerswyck, near Albany. The Van Rensselaer patroonship survived the English conquest and the American Revolution.

Ordinary Dutchmen received no such lordly inducements to emigrate. In an effort to increase the tiny flow of settlers, the company issued a more liberal charter in 1640, granting 200 acres to those transporting five persons. But the free land policy which rapidly peopled New England was never followed in Dutch New Netherland or the successor colony of English New York.

The men chosen to govern New Netherland were quarrelsome, arrogant and unimaginative. Wouter Van Twiller, the second governor, was fresh from a clerk's desk at Dutch West India House. He could not cope with hostile officials. Next came Willem Kieft, an Amsterdam merchant who failed in handling the Indians of the lower Hudson Valley. These tribes had sought refuge from Mohawk onslaughts among the Dutch in Jersey and the Manhattan area, but Kieft treacherously ordered them slaughtered. Inevitable Indian reprisals brought terror and destruction to settlements around New York. Before peace was established, most of the settlers south of Albany had to retire behind a wall built across Manhattan Island, which later gave Wall Street its name.

Although the Dutch had refused to give the settlers a voice in the government, at the height of the Indian fighting Kieft finally had to seek counsel from groups chosen by the townsmen and farmers. The implacable opposition of one of these committees ended the rule of the thoroughly detested and discredited Kieft. His successor in 1647, the one-legged hero, Peter Stuyvesant, was the only Dutch governor who put the public good ahead of self-interest. But Stuyvesant was a vitriolic and humorless man whose minor concessions to self-government were too little and too late.

I N the 25 years following 1648, England and Holland fought three wars, all sparked by fierce commercial rivalry. During one of these conflicts, four English frigates entered New York harbor in August 1664. The frenzied efforts of Stuyvesant failed to rally support from the people of New Amsterdam. Resistance, his burghers told him, was "nothing less than to gape before an oven." Stuyvesant had to surrender, and the city was renamed New York. In 1673-1674 the Dutch briefly reoccupied it. Otherwise, the English kept the colony until the end of the Revolution in 1783.

Two unfortunate Dutch policies—monopoly of land and government by the

Peter Stuyvesant, last Dutch director-general of New Amsterdam, defiantly rips up a surrender summons from the British in 1664. Stuyvesant, who 20 years before had lost a leg fighting the Portuguese in the West Indies, stayed in Manhattan under the British until his death eight years later.

The silver Pine Tree shilling, usually about the size of the present U.S. quarter, was issued by the first colonial mint, opened in Boston in 1652. It represented an effort to provide a uniform coinage in place of the jumble of European coins then in use. The die for the shillings was never changed and so, though issued for 30 years, the date on them remained the same.

few—continued under the English governors who ruled in the name of James, Duke of York, proprietor of the colony. Huge estates went to the governors and their favorites. Newly created English manor lords now vied for social position with the Old Dutch patroons. Men-on-the-make like the young Scot, Robert Livingston, quickly carved out huge empires. As secretary of Indian affairs in the frontier trading post of Albany, Livingston exploited his official sources of trade information and improved his rank in society by marrying the widow of a Van Rensselaer. "Beginning being a little Book keeper," commented one harsh critic on Livingston's activities, "he has screwed himself into one of the most considerable estates in the province." Such land-grabbing left a long heritage of agrarian unrest and landlord-tenant animosity.

Government too was still monopolized by the few. The Duke's Laws, the colony's first code, was an exception; this was adopted in 1665 by deputies chosen by the towns. But when urged to set up a legislative body, James II, then Duke of York, declared in 1676 that assemblies "would be of dangerous consequence, nothing being more knowne than the aptness of such bodyes to assume to themselves many priviledges which prove destructive." In 1683 New York's first Irish Catholic governor, Thomas Dongan, summoned delegates who enacted a Charter of Liberties and Privileges providing for regular assemblies. But when James became king in 1685, he rescinded the legislation of the assembly and ended its meetings.

Englishmen did not suffer such deprivation of their liberties without protest. The Revolution of 1688 in England touched off a rebellion in New York led by a German settler, Jacob Leisler. Governor Francis Nicholson fled. William and Mary, after coming to the throne, named Henry Sloughter governor. When Sloughter arrived in 1691, he tried the chief rebels for treason and hanged Leisler and one of his lieutenants, Jacob Milborne. However, Sloughter did summon an assembly, and New York joined the other colonies in having representative government.

The former Dutch colony had included the area between the Delaware Bay and the Atlantic now called New Jersey. This tract was granted to John Lord Berkeley and Sir George Carteret in 1665 by the Duke of York. Subsequently the Berkeley (East Jersey) and Carteret (West Jersey) interests were sold to groups of Quakers, including William Penn. East Jersey attracted Puritans from New England and later, Lowland Scots and Scotch-Irish. West Jersey saw the real beginnings of colonization by the English Quakers, soon to found Pennsylvania on the opposite shore of the Delaware River.

OF the original Thirteen Colonies, none owed as much to the extraordinary vision and practical genius of one man as Pennsylvania to William Penn. An Oxford-educated aristocrat, Penn left the licentious Court of Charles II and abandoned the Church of England to embrace the faith of the persecuted Society of Friends, or Quakers. This radical Protestant group carried to extreme lengths the insistence on private judgment in matters of religion. The English Quakers had an itch for martyrdom, preferring to give their lives for the truth rather than live with a half-truth. Many suffered the whipping post and jail. Penn was himself imprisoned and in his cell wrote "No Cross, No Crown," an eloquent statement of his religious convictions. In 1681 Charles II, to pay off his long-standing debt to the young Quaker's father, the late Admiral Sir William Penn, granted a huge tract of land to Penn who had served out

his sentence. This was named Pennsylvania (or Penn's Woods) in honor of the admiral, a naval hero. The following year the Duke of York transferred to Penn the territory known as Delaware.

Possessing these fertile lands, Penn could carry out his "Holy Experiment," gratifying both his proprietary ambitions and humanitarian impulses. The preface to the colony's constitution, Penn's "Frame of Government" of 1682, stated that "Any Government is free to the People under it (whatever be the Frame) where the Laws rule, and the People are a Party to those Laws." Because these principles were adhered to, Pennsylvania and Delaware remained free governments. Penn spent only 22 months in the colony on his first visit. In that brief time he saw to the laying out of Philadelphia, the permanent establishment of the colony's government, the negotiation of long-term peace with the Indians, and the launching of a campaign to attract immigrants from the Continent and Ireland as well as England.

WHEN the new monarchs, William and Mary, came to the throne after the Glorious Revolution of 1688, they were suspicious of William Penn because of his friendship with James II, the last Stuart king, and the crown took over the colony between 1692 and 1694. Thereafter Penn and his heirs owned it until the American Revolution. Despite its striking prosperity, Pennsylvania even in Penn's own day was racked by party division. "For the love of God, me, and the poor country," Penn implored, "be not so governmentish, so noisy, and open, in your dissatisfactions." While the conservative proprietary party managed to fend off the antiproprietary faction for many years, the refusal of the Quakers to compromise on the question of arms for defense cost them control of the government.

"All they that take the sword shall perish with the sword" was a fundamental Quaker tenet. Penn, himself a pacifist, distinguished between aggressive and defensive wars, implying that the latter might be justified. His followers were more rigid. In the early intercolonial wars the Quaker assembly refused to enact military laws, and gave the war effort only indirect financial aid. Most of the settlers on the exposed frontiers were German and Scotch-Irish pioneers who did not share the pacifism of Quaker Philadelphia, and the issue came to a head in the French and Indian War with the shocking defeat of British General Braddock's troops in 1755. Braddock, with some 2,100 troops, had marched into the forest to attack the French at Fort Duquesne, on the site of present-day Pittsburgh. Ignoring the advice of his colonial officers, including George Washington, Braddock followed European military tactics and his force was cut to pieces. The rout of the redcoats by French and Indian forces spread panic on the frontier. Forced to choose between keeping their religious principles or the reins of government, the Quaker leaders withdrew from the assembly, leaving non-Quakers in command.

With increasing prosperity, the center of Pennsylvania Quaker life tended to shift from meetinghouse to countinghouse. Despite their growing conservatism, Pennsylvania's Quakers still showed enthusiasm for a broad range of humanitarian movements. They opposed capital punishment and slavery; they advocated prison reform and the building of hospitals and insane asylums. And the sectarian humanity of William Penn and his Quakers was to be complemented by the cosmopolitan enlightenment of Benjamin Franklin, Philadelphia's greatest citizen of the 18th Century.

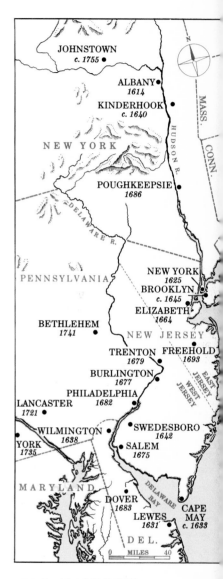

THE MIDDLE COLONIES' GRADUAL SETTLEMENT

The upper Hudson River had access to the rich fur trade, so the Dutch founded Albany before settling New Amsterdam (now New York). Swedes moved in around Delaware Bay. Both nations lost out when England plugged the gap between its northern and southern colonies. Settlements such as Elizabeth bloomed in New Jersey. The Quakers founded Burlington and Philadelphia, and later encouraged German immigrants to settle the Pennsylvania Dutch villages of Lancaster, York and Bethlehem. Far to the north the fur traders pushed on up to Johnstown.

VOWING to uphold their own laws, 41 Pilgrim "Saints" and Anglican "Strangers" sign the Mayflower Compact in Provincetown harbor, November 11, 1620. Then they explored several sites for settlement.

The austere world of the Puritans

O N December 21, 1620, when the Pilgrims began coming ashore at Plymouth, they had already committed an act as momentous as any that lay ahead of them. Aboard ship they had signed (*above*) the Mayflower Compact: "We ... solemnly and mutually in the Presence of God ... covenant and combine ourselves ... into a civil Body Politick." They pledged full obedience to all decisions made for the general good. In effect, this simple document established democratic self-government, with church law as the sole code and constitution of an incorporated business community. Thus was created the first "Biblical Commonwealth" in New England.

Soon other Puritan groups in England were making similar agreements. The fiery Thomas Hooker exhorted his flock: "England hath seen her best dayes, and now evill dayes are befalling us; God is packing up his Gospell, because no body will buy his wares, nor come to his price. . . . He is going, stop him, and let not Thy God depart. . . ." The Puritans did not let their God depart alone. After failing to "purify" the Church of England from within, they had withdrawn into their own congregations which interpreted Scriptures and worshiped according to conscience; and now, to escape persecution, they separated themselves from their homeland. Many of them set sail believing that in time England, purged of religious pomp and corruption, would welcome them back and embrace their unadorned faith. None of them dreamed of how profoundly they themselves would change while practicing God's Word in the wilderness.

"LANDING OF THE PILGRIMS," painted in 1901, imaginatively depicts Captain Miles Standish (right), a hired professional soldier, lending a hand to his wife Rose as she steps ashore at Plymouth. Shunning the "pagan" festivities of Christmas, the Pilgrims observed December 25, 1620, by commencing to build their colony in an open field between the forest and the sea.

"Many more godly freinds and Christian brethren"

IN the early years at Plymouth, the Pilgrims were sorely tried by hunger and epidemic, biting cold and grinding hard labor. As William Bradford, their second governor, said of earlier hardships, they "looked not much on those things, but lift[ed] up their eyes to the heavens . . . and quieted their spirits." Soon, Bradford noted, "Many more godly freinds and Christian brethren" were arriving in flight from increasing persecution, which meant "a larger harvest unto ye Lord." By 1630 the Puritans of the Massachusetts Bay Colony had settlements at Weymouth, Salem and Boston. By 1640, the New England coast sheltered over 25,000 enterprising immigrants.

Always the Scriptures were in the forefront of the Puritans' minds, the Sabbath service at the heart of their week, the meetinghouse at the center of their spartan towns. Their God was the stern God of the Old Testament. Their severe Calvinistic doctrines permitted no priestly robes, no crucifixes, no kneeling, no "Devil's bagpipes" (organs). Energetic, impassive, austere, hostile to compromise, they went their way secure in the belief that this life was merely a rehearsal for the hereafter.

Churchgoing Pilgrims wear somber clothing given them by a

INVESTIGATING IMMORALITY at Quincy, 30 miles from the Plymouth colony, a band of Pilgrims *(foreground)* catches its neighbors "quaffing . . . dancing and frisking" around a pagan Maypole. Shocked, the Pilgrims chopped down the pole, seized the "lord of misrule," Anglican aristocrat Thomas Morton, and sent him to England on charges of trading arms to the Indians.

misinformed artist in this 19th Century work. In fact, they were not dowdy; they followed current fashions but used color in moderation.

RATIONING FOOD, a Pilgrim elder tries to make 10 bushels of Indian corn last through the first winter at Plymouth. By April 1621, half of the colonists had died of the "General Sickness."

ATTACKING INDIANS, Pilgrims led by Miles Standish kill seven braves at Weymouth. The raid frustrated an uprising, warned rival colonies that the pious Pilgrims could also be ruthless.

A challenge to authority
and a crisis of superstition

IN the Puritan fusion of church and state, ministers interpreted Scriptures officially, and judges applied these opinions as divine law. Though elected, these officials perpetuated their power by restricting the vote to stockholders in the corporate colony, and by admitting few new stockholders. Dissenters had to conform or move on. As early as 1636, Thomas Hooker's congregation left Boston for Hartford. The same year, Roger Williams, banished from Boston, began a new settlement at Providence. He later wrote of his tormentors, "Yourselves pretend [to] liberty of conscience, but alas! it is but self, the great god self, only to yourselves."

Brutal punishment failed to force a "gospel-glutted" generation to toe the line of righteousness. Opposition mounted in spite of the flogging and even the hanging of particular Quakers and Baptists. It was largely to bolster their sagging authority that late in the 17th Century, ministers led by Increase and Cotton Mather revived and exploited the people's fear of witchcraft. But after the hysteria of 1692, when some 150 "witches" were tried in Salem, Puritan power continued to wane.

GALLOWS HILL is marked by a gaunt oak. Here, during three months of Salem trials in 1692, nineteen victims were executed as witches and buried without ceremony in common graves.

A CHARGE OF WITCHCRAFT is lodged against George Jacobs (*kneeling at right*), by a group of Salem girls, one of them writhing (*left foreground*) to prove she is "possessed" by the accused.

90

Jacobs, condemned by the court, was hanged on August 19, 1692. Soon after, the witch-hunting fever burned itself out, to be replaced by public grief and repentance. Twelve jurors confessed their error in heeding "spectral evidence." Accepting the "shame and blame" for his part in the trials, Judge Samuel Sewall devoted a day each year to penitent prayer and fasting.

The persistent heritage of the Puritan spirit

MINISTER Richard Mather is starkly portrayed in this wood-cut, the first in America. His descendants included 80 clerics, of whom the most powerful were Cotton and Increase Mather.

FOR all of its high purpose and ardent sincerity, Puritanism perpetuated some of the same intolerances its faithful had emigrated to escape. On the eve of the Revolution, there was a growing rejection of orthodox Puritanism. Yet even after Puritanism died as a political force, its culture remained deeply ingrained in American life. Puritan radicals had challenged the traditional authority of kings and bishops, had shaken old and rigid social attitudes, had asserted the primacy of individual conscience and the virtues of personal initiative. Reaction to Puritanism helped shape early American political parties and helped produce the constitutional separation of church and state. Puritan desire for learning led to the enactment of laws for compulsory public education and to the establishment of Harvard (below) and other colleges. The ethical zeal of Puritanism suffused the intellectual revival of 19th Century New England, contributing to the idealistic philosophy of Ralph Waldo Emerson and the dour, brooding novels of Nathaniel Hawthorne and Herman Melville. The Puritan character, although diluted as teachers and traders from New England spread throughout the country, is still reflected in the character of the modern American—in his sense of the moral content of life, in his mixture of hardheaded practicality and militant zeal for humanitarian causes.

HARVARD COLLEGE perpetuates the tradition of learning espoused by the Puritans. Founded only 16 years after the landing at Plymouth, Harvard is seen below as it appeared in 1740.

RUGGED MEETINGHOUSE (opposite) erected in 1681 is still in use in Hingham, Massachusetts. Its Puritan simplicity represents the first native American contribution to architecture.

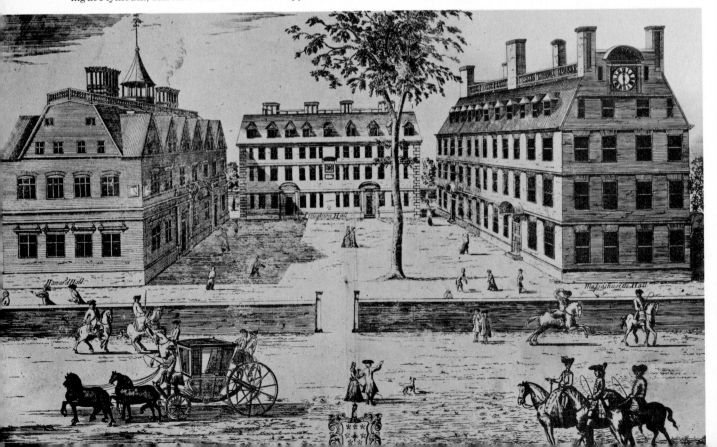

5. A PEOPLE
AT WORK

THOUGH it was quickly apparent to the early settlers that America offered breathing space for the cramped peoples of Europe, no one could guess how rapidly the vast unsettled wilderness would be tamed. At first, populating the colonies had been slow and arduous. Beset by famine, disease and hostile Indians, Englishmen arriving in Jamestown and Plymouth were lucky to survive at all. But by 1641, largely because of the great Puritan migration from Europe, some 50,000 English settlers had reached North America. Seventy-five years later, the continuous outpouring of emigrants from Europe and the British Isles had brought the colonial population to 435,000. In 1775, on the eve of the Revolution, 2.5 million people had a personal stake in the Thirteen Colonies—roughly a third as many as inhabited all Great Britain.

Most immigrants lived on the land. In 1790, the first federal census found less than 3 per cent of the population in towns of more than 10,000. But towns and cities were flourishing. Philadelphia and its environs, with 54,000 inhabitants, was the first city in size. New York was second with 33,100; Boston, with 18,300, third; Charleston, the largest city of the South, numbered 16,400. The townsmen of these and smaller communities like New Haven, Norfolk and Baltimore had an impact on trade, crafts, and political and intellectual activity that far exceeded their numbers.

Immigration steadily increased but a good part of the population growth came from a surplus of births over deaths. Families were large in the colonial

FARM WIFE'S WORKROOM is reconstructed in this kitch-
n of an 18th Century New York house. Women spun,
yed and wove yarns like those hanging from the ceiling.

period. They had to be because infant mortality rates were high. Children's diseases like measles and diphtheria took a heavy toll. Epidemics of small-pox, typhoid and yellow fever decimated new settlements. But many who survived to maturity developed some immunity to disease and achieved a life span that does not compare too unfavorably with that of our own times.

"By the sweat of thy brow thou shalt eat thy bread," colonial children laboriously wrote in their copybooks. And in truth, for everyone—young or old, longtime settler or immigrant green off the boat—there was much work to be done and never enough hands to do it. American almanacs of the 18th Century were studded with aphorisms about the sinfulness of being unemployed. Labor was always in short supply. Every contemporary authority agrees on the relatively high wages in the colonies. Governor Winthrop of Massachusetts tells of one master who had been obliged to sell a pair of oxen to pay his employee. Then he informed the workman that he saw no chance of being able to continue to pay him. "Sell more cattle," the workman advised. "What shall I do when they are gone?" the master asked. "You can serve me and get them back," was the reply. Pioneer entrepreneurs, in what became an almost ritual lament, bewailed the high cost of wages: "The servants will be masters," they said, "and the masters servants." And often it was true.

LAND was cheap, and if an artisan disliked his work he could mark out a farmstead and become his own master. The result was an economic paradox. High wages induced European workmen to emigrate. But at the same time it was the high wage scale that made it possible for them to afford land and turn to farming. Colonial authorities, confronted with soaring wages and a constant shortage of hands, instituted controls adapted from English legislation. Anyone living "without a calling" was compelled to work or be punished as a criminal. Idlers were whipped, fined, put out at forced labor or committed to the workhouse. Despite all this, the labor shortage continued.

Almost from the beginning the colonies took measures to control wages and prices. A ceiling was set on wages and a floor was placed under hours of employment. In Massachusetts the General Court first fixed wage scales for the colony and then turned regulation over to the towns. Enforcement was buttressed by the churches, which exercised a stern censorship over the behavior of their congregations in everything from business ethics, intemperance and Sabbathbreaking to gambling and "mixed [male and female] dancings."

Such regulations, to have been effective, should have been coordinated and enforced throughout all thirteen colonies. They were not. Workers who felt themselves underpaid in one locality could and did move on to another where higher wages prevailed. As a result, wage and price fixing on a broad basis gradually disintegrated as the 18th Century advanced.

Largely because a worker could get the terms he wanted by his own efforts, no permanent labor unions emerged in the colonial and Revolutionary periods. When workers and producers did take concerted action, it was usually for special reasons. Master workers in some trades combined to keep others from entering their trades, but even restraints of this kind decreased throughout the 18th Century. Licensed tradesmen—porters, carters, chimney sweeps, bakers and innkeepers, whose services affected the public interest—joined to get better fees or prices from the local regulating authorities. Sometimes, bound servants (employees bound by strict contract for specified periods)

Gentleness was not the rule in British jails, as this scene of an 18th Century debtors prison shows. Inmates were at the mercy of "cruell and implacable Jaylors, being . . . men of austere and inhumane conditions. . . ." From these prisons, "distinguished for their filth and bad ventilation," came many people who were paroled to work and begin a new life in the colonies.

went on strike, demonstrated or conspired to break their contract of employment. Occurrences of this sort were most common in the tobacco provinces, particularly in the 1600s. The authorities usually stopped them quickly.

In the crafts, where white labor, especially in the southern colonies, came to suffer from the competition of Negro slaves set up in trade by their masters, "combinations" were formed to keep blacks out. But the slaveowners and the government were unsympathetic, holding that this interfered with a slaveowner's right to use his property as he wished. Such conflict between labor and authority was rare. White journeymen seldom struck for better conditions, but their right to strike was rarely actually challenged. In the 1700s master craftsmen, particularly house carpenters, had no difficulty forming groups to fix prices and wages, and "friendly" societies were organized for social and philanthropic ends. In England these "box clubs," as they were called, were harassed as blinds for conspiratorial labor agitation. In colonial America the power of such societies and other labor combinations did not inspire the counterpressure which might have driven labor to serious organization.

Down to the end of the 18th Century the vast majority of workmen for America's labor market was voluntarily recruited under the bound labor system. Because there were no trade schools in the colonies, nor were there any technical high schools, orphan asylums or foster homes, apprenticeship was the one practical way to relieve the community of the burden of supporting orphans and to enable parents to provide their children a technical education. With the consent of his parent, guardian or the local officials, an apprentice bound himself to serve a master from four to seven years and sometimes longer. Apprenticeships normally ran until the age of 21 for boys and 16 or 18 for girls. The apprentice came under the discipline of the master and his household, learned his master's trade and received some rudiments of education. Many masters, themselves illiterate, could not instruct their apprentices in the three Rs, so the practice grew up of sending the young people to night schools for one quarter's schooling every year. This did not encroach on the apprentice's regular working hours.

In colonial times, the possession of "black beavor" hats gave status to the wearers and provided work for a considerable number of hatters. One of the processes, a final ironing that produced a high gloss, is shown above. By 1731, colonial hat production had climbed to 10,000 a year, and American hats were being worn in many sections of the New World and Europe.

L‌ARGE numbers of adult workers agreed to emigrate as "redemptioners," who redeemed by labor in America the cost of passage across the Atlantic —an average of £10 to £12. The recruiting agent made them sign indentures, usually requiring four years of bound labor. The agent then assigned the indentures to the ship's captain, who "sold" the passengers on their arrival at a colonial port. Aggressive recruiters sent drummers to the inland English towns to advertise the voyages to America and distribute extravagantly optimistic literature. After signing up the emigrant, the agent might confine him on land or actually imprison him aboard ship until sailing time. Unscrupulous agents were not above kidnaping children or "trapanning" (ensnaring) adults. One contemporary ballad pointed a matrimonial moral:

> Beware you scolding wives, if no fair means will win ye,
> Lest that your Husbands you entrap, and send you to Virginny.

The colonies received a large number of convicts. Parliament had authorized the transportation overseas of "rogues, vagabonds, and sturdy beggars," along with convicted felons whose sentences were commuted to seven- or 14-year terms of servitude. Some 50,000 convicts were shipped, principally to

Maryland and Virginia. Colonial governments protested, but poor farmers along the frontier snapped up cheap convict indentures, for they could not afford more costly redemptioners or the still more expensive slaves. A good deal of sentimental nonsense has been written about such convicts. Since few people will admit to a convict ancestor, there is a persistent myth that they were really not criminals, but poor debtors and political prisoners. In fact, many transported convicts had been found guilty of murder, rape, highway robbery, burglary, horse- and sheepstealing, and grand larceny. A smaller number was sentenced for minor thefts like shoplifting goods worth as little as sixpence. Among the motley ranks were women like "Princess Susanna Carolina Matilda, Marchioness of Waldegrave," a gaudy individual who gave Philadelphia society some embarrassing moments when she was revealed to be plain Sarah Wilson, transported for the theft of royal jewels.

Some convicts, however, managed to bury their pasts in the New World, eventually becoming substantial citizens. Anthony Lamb, who was convicted in 1724 as an accomplice of the notorious thief Jack Sheppard, was sentenced to transportation to Virginia for seven years. Completing his term, he went to Philadelphia, where he thrived as a maker of mathematical instruments. Then he moved to New York, married respectably and became a solid tradesman. His son John, a prosperous merchant, became a leading figure among the Sons of Liberty and a general in the Continental army.

A BOUT the last of August came in a Dutch man of warre that sold us twenty negars." Thus concisely did John Rolfe, founder of commercial tobacco cultivation in Virginia, report the first importation in 1619 of Negroes from Africa. Slavery was not invented in the English colonies. For nearly two centuries before the settlement of Virginia, a trade in slaves had been carried on along the West African coast. As the English empire expanded to the New World, slave traders saw a chance for profit in this business. Slave traffic became an integral part of a colonial commercial pattern, known as the "triangular trade," which operated between New England, Africa and the West Indies or the Southern colonies. New England rum, guns and gunpowder, utensils, textiles and food were offered to West African chiefs in return for slaves. The human cargo was packed aboard ship, chained together by twos, with hardly any room to stand, lie or sit down. During the voyages that sometimes lasted as long as 14 weeks, there were often epidemics that increased death rates alarmingly, but profits from the slave trade remained attractively high.

Colonial taverns were required in some places to "sett up some inoffensive sign . . ." such as those above and below. Aside from the church, the tavern was the most important public institution and, in some colonies, towns lacking one were subject to fines. Some taverns had only a few beds, and travelers commonly found themselves bedded on the taproom floor.

At first such blacks were treated as bound servants in the colonies and were freed when their terms expired, with a chance to make their own way in a fairly egalitarian society. But there probably were not more than a few hundred of these cases. Sometime in the course of the 1640s, the practice began of selling imported blacks as servants for life. By the 1660s, statutes in Virginia and Maryland had given slavery a hereditary legal status.

For the South, this decision to deny blacks the status of white servants was fateful. The Tidewater plantation system consisted of large farms, from several hundred to many thousands of acres, on which a single crop was cultivated by large groups of workers and sold to merchants. Growers of such plantation crops as tobacco, indigo and rice said they needed an assured supply of labor, able to stand the heat. But those who justified slavery on this ground ignored the fact that the need could have been just as well supplied with white

bound servants except for the inconvenience of having to replace redeemed workers or runaway servants. The institution, once established, became self-perpetuating as Southerners grew used to its workings.

By 1775 the stepped-up slave trade, along with a natural increase of population, had brought the number of blacks in America to a half million. More than three fifths of these were in Virginia and the Carolinas. In South Carolina the slave population actually exceeded the white. Some colonies imposed prohibitive duties on the slave trade, not from humanitarian considerations but in fear of a huge, unmanageable black population. British slave traders, however, brought pressure on the home government to abrogate those duties.

Scattered voices cried out against slavery in colonial times. Many Quakers opposed the practice from the beginning and John Woolman, a New Jersey Quaker leader, warned in 1760 that the consequences of slavery would be "War and Desolation." Quakers ceased buying slaves and began freeing those they owned. In 1775 Tom Paine, soon to enter the wider arena of Revolutionary pamphleteering, advocated "an act of continental legislation, which shall put a stop to the importation of Negroes for sale, soften the hard fate of those already here, and in time procure their freedom." Not until the Revolution was won, however, would there be the germ of a program for the gradual modification of the "peculiar institution."

Most colonists—rich and poor, free and slave, Englishman and Continental European—were firmly attached to the land. The land was cheap if not free.

That was the most important fact about colonial farming. Despite the so-called land aristocracy established in Maryland and Carolina, America never had an organized feudal system. The United States is a country that has had no Middle Ages. This fact has left its incisive mark on American history. Unlike the countries of Europe, America never knew either the pageantry of absolute monarchy or the separation of a ruling class from the populace on the basis of some mystical superiority of lineage. The ceremonials of hereditary office, the privileges based on ancient relationships of lord and vassal, were largely absent. To this happy omission, Americans owe their relative lack of rigid class lines. And when the time came to cut the cord with the mother country, there was no powerful group of nobles to object, no close ties of custom to be cut before a new form of government could be established.

Fancy or plain, wigs were all the rage. Following European trends, every fashionable colonist wore one. Even some slaves had wigs. The finer ones were quite expensive, and offers of rewards for the return of stolen wigs were common. Early wigs were curly and long, but the knotted wig (above) and the bag wig (below) harmonized with neater wig fashions.

THE fertility and availability of virgin soil permitted the most improvident farming methods, although colonial farmers were no worse than most European or contemporary Indian farmers in their wasteful techniques. When the Indians could not find a cleared fertile spot, they made space in the forest by cutting away the bark of trees with stone axes and then burning around the roots. The dead trees were left standing until they fell. The smaller trees were cut down. The colonists followed their example. In the mid-18th Century Jared Eliot, a New England clergyman, physician and natural scientist, explained the advantages of planting turnips, clovers and grasses to restore the fertility of the soil. It was years before anyone paid much attention to his advice. The soil in the colonies was usually tilled year after year until it "ran out," although here and there, regular rotation of crops was practiced.

The tools used by colonial farmers were only slightly better than those of the Indians. Plows were scarce in the early years, and those which eventually came into wide use were made of wood, with only the plowshare of iron. It

took a strong team, usually heavy oxen, to pull such a plow. Farmers cut grain with sickles or scythes, threshing it with wooden flails or by having oxen trample it out, methods little advanced over those of Biblical times.

In New England, farmers had to cultivate boulder-strewn land unsuited to plantation agriculture. Long, severe winters and short summers limited the area to a single crop a year, and even that could be ruined by an early frost. Except for the Connecticut, New England rivers were swift-flowing streams, which, though they later furnished useful water power for the textile mills, did not provide the navigable waterways so essential for interior transportation. By and large, shipping crops to market was difficult and expensive.

Confronted by such obstacles, the first New England pioneers settled in groups and raised crops for their own subsistence. This arrangement fitted the character of their emigration, which was customarily carried on by religious congregations or by people from the same neighborhood, often with close family ties. These settlements were encouraged by the Massachusetts General Court, which granted free land to groups provided they made certain improvements and set aside land for common use. Grants were generally made for 36 square miles (a land measure later adopted for the rectangular surveys of the United States public lands). Thus began the township system, so important later in the opening of the American West.

While the court's intention may have been to give the land to the town, it was more often than not granted to a group of proprietors, who controlled land distribution within the town. In turn, acreage was allotted to individual freeholders on the basis of the size of a man's original investment in the enterprise, the number of people in his family and any special skills he might have which could be useful to the community. For the most part, land was distributed fairly. Each family normally received a town lot of three to five acres together with a number of small patches of outlying lands. Total family holdings ranged from 50 to 200 acres, only a small portion of which were arable. In the 18th Century the descendants of original grantees, called "commoners," were generally able to establish their exclusive legal right to the ownership of such lands as were still undistributed. New arrivals, the "noncommoners," either had to buy land from a commoner or move farther out to

a frontier settlement. This restrictive land policy speeded the expansion of New England and pushed the westward migration of late-comers.

The New England village economy was modeled on that of the medieval English farming communities. The common, or pasture land, was available to all freeholders, as it was in English manors. And New England adopted the medieval three-field system in which one field lay fallow, the second was planted with wheat (or corn) and rye, and the third with barley, oats, peas and beans. Indian corn, easily cultivated by hand, was the favorite crop. Wheat, which was first raised in the fertile Connecticut Valley, could be grown only after the fields had been thoroughly plowed. South of New England, the fertile lands between the Hudson and the Potomac soon became the most fruitful area for general farming along the entire Atlantic Seaboard. There the soil lent itself easily to the plow. Wheat instead of corn was the major staple, but rye, oats, barley and other cereals, along with potatoes, grew in abundance. Unlike New England, where subsistence farming prevailed, these "bread colonies" were able to market a large part of their crops.

A long growing season and the plantation system made the colonial South the rich center of commercial agriculture where staples were raised primarily for market. The assembling of the large tracts needed for plantations was made feasible by the headright system, by which the planter got 50 acres for every worker he imported from abroad. Since capital was needed to bring over an immigrant, the system favored those with cash or connections. By the 18th Century, however, headrights could be bought for cash, which meant that land could be acquired without importing labor.

Farming in the Tidewater South was capitalistic rather than subsistence. The planter raised a specialized crop for export—in Maryland and Virginia tobacco, in South Carolina rice and indigo. He himself did not work the soil but employed an overseer who managed the labor. His economy was highly sensitive to the world price of his staple and he became largely dependent upon credit advanced by merchants in England and Scotland. Credit enabled him to purchase new land as his soil became exhausted, helped maintain the large labor supply that plantation farming demanded, and supported that conspicuously high standard of living which his social position dictated.

The prototypes of classified advertising were items such as these which often appeared in colonial newspapers. Because transportation was so slow, all but the local news was weeks or even months late. The editors of these early papers seldom wrote their own editorials, but made use of letters and essays by local gentlemen of leisure, discussing current issues.

In the lower South, plantations took on a West Indian character. With the introduction of irrigation methods around 1724, rice, originally grown only near inland swamps, spread to the tidal marshes. Indentured servants sickened in the hot pestilential swamplands; slaves were better acclimated. During the worst of the summer season, planters moved to healthier locations, leaving management entirely to overseers. Once the West Indies turned from indigo to more profitable sugar, the blue-dye plant became an important crop of South Carolina plantations. Although sea-island cotton, prized for its long fibers, was cultivated in Georgia as early as 1767, and short-staple cotton was grown in scattered areas before the Revolution, cotton did not become the major plantation crop until the introduction of the cotton gin in 1793. Nonetheless, by 1776, South Carolina was producing nearly one million pounds a year.

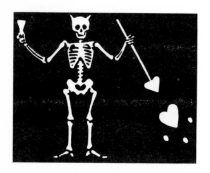

Bedecked with weapons, Edward "Blackbeard" Teach (below) stands ready to fight. His awesome reputation made him greatly feared by ship captains. But he had a fondness for women and it is said he had 14 wives. In 1718, his "Jolly Roger" (above) was pulled down when Lieutenant Robert Maynard caught him, cut off the hairy head and displayed it on his bowsprit.

TRANSATLANTIC trade, which deeply influenced colonial economy, was shaken in the 17th Century by the fierce rivalry between England and Holland. Over the years Holland had become the transshipment point for trade between central Europe and the rest of the world, and Amsterdam outranked every other seaport. Products from all over the world went through it, paying Dutch commissions, insurance, warehouse fees and freight. For a time, religious and civil strife at home prevented England from challenging Dutch commercial pre-eminence. But once Cromwell had crushed the Royalists, he began building a strong navy. Then England was ready to fight Holland—but not by underbidding for cargoes and freights. Instead, legislation was enacted to restrict foreign competition and to make sure that the trade to and from the English colonies would supplement rather than compete with the home economy. Three Anglo-Dutch wars between 1652 and 1674 established England's supremacy on the seas and assured the success of her international trade program.

The shape of the colonial trade program was set by a series of shipping and trade laws, passed during the years from 1651 to 1767. The entire complex of legislation is usually known by the name of the Navigation Acts passed in 1650 and 1651. These provided that no goods could be imported from Asia, Africa or America into England, Ireland or the colonies, except in ships owned and in major part manned by Englishmen. To strike at Holland's middleman trade, the acts forbade direct importation by any part of the empire of any European goods except in English ships or in ships of the producing nation.

The colonies angrily opposed these acts and insisted that they would continue to trade with the Dutch. But the English laws became more and more restrictive. Soon no goods could be exported from any English colony except in ships owned and manned by Englishmen. Certain specified (or "enumerated") articles of American growth or manufacture could be shipped only to England or her other colonies. By the act of 1660 the "enumerated" list included sugar, tobacco and indigo. It grew longer as colonial commerce expanded. The last of these acts, in 1767, required that all goods shipped by the colonies to any part of Europe north of Spain had to go to England first.

Because smuggling reached a high point along the Atlantic Coast in the wake of the Molasses Act of 1733, an impression long persisted that the Navigation Acts were not effectively enforced. This was not the case. Ships sailing from the colonies had to post a bond that was forfeited if they violated any regulations, and naval officers and customs commissioners enforced the laws. For the act of 1696 had already tightened the enforcement procedure

and voided all colonial laws which were contrary to the Navigation Acts.

The pressures generated by the Navigation Acts forced merchants to invent patterns of overseas commerce to help correct New England's unfavorable balance of trade with England. Variations on the triangular trade were developed to pay for imported manufactured goods from England, principally textiles and hardware. For example, New England fish and lumber, or flour from the Middle Colonies, were shipped to the West Indies in exchange for sugar and molasses. The second leg of the journey carried the sugar and molasses to London or Bristol; the last leg brought English goods back to America. Alternatively, on the second leg, West Indian rum was exchanged in West Africa for slaves, who were brought back to the colonies for sale.

Even without the various shipping and trade acts, buying and selling across the seas was a risky business. Ships were small; the sea was vast and dangerous. Until marine insurance became readily available in the colonies about the middle of the 18th Century, all damages from wind and weather usually had to be borne by the shipowner himself. Pirates were another problem. Originally, freebooting had been regarded as a patriotic enterprise. English buccaneers had looted the Spanish treasure fleets for Queen Elizabeth. Later Henry Morgan, operating from the Caribbean, ravaged the Spanish Main. Instead of being convicted of piracy, he became an English national hero, was knighted, became acting governor of Jamaica and ended his days there.

The colonists were of two minds about piracy. Though they passed laws that punished piracy with death, they welcomed freebooters in their ports because they came to replenish supplies and paid in needed silver and gold coin. As piracy increased, Parliament also made the crime a capital offense. Under the act of 1699, a New York sea captain of Scottish origin named Captain William Kidd was convicted in London and hanged at Wapping. The legend lives on that he successfully buried most of his treasure, and romantics have been searching the highlands of the lower Hudson River and dredging the coves and inlets of Long Island Sound ever since in futile efforts to find the loot.

Many pirates took advantage of a general amnesty offered by the crown in 1717 to retire with a whole skin. Stede Bonnet was caught and executed. Edward Teach, the feared "Blackbeard," was killed in an attack by a Virginia expedition. And the notorious woman buccaneer, Mary Read, died in jail. From the early 18th Century, during the years of sporadic war that England waged against France and Spain, shipowners turned to privateering. This was an arrangement by which the government authorized private armed merchant vessels to attack and seize enemy ships in wartime. Privateering became a big business, and in colonies like New York, impressive fortunes were built from prizes seized, quite legally, by the use of force.

COLONIAL businessmen were continually hampered by a shortage of hard money and inadequate credit. In the early days they had engaged in barter, exchanging manufactured goods for staple commodities. In Maryland and Virginia, tobacco crop notes (negotiable receipts for tobacco in warehouses) became acceptable currency. But everybody wanted to accumulate hard cash in the form of foreign coinage or "plate." The favorite method was to put a premium on such money in order to lure it from the chests of pirates and other holders of gold and silver. Britain tried to put a ceiling on such overvaluation of foreign money, but as Governor Hunter of New York observed, "'Tis not in

The colonial mariner was a respected member of the profitable seaman's calling. A sailor could pick up trade items at ports of call and sell them at great profit, and any American cabin boy could aspire to become a captain and own his ship. With these possibilities as lures, many boys gladly traded a tedious life on the farm for a dangerous but exciting one at sea.

the power of men or angels to beat the people . . . out of a silly notion . . . of the value of plate."

Eventually the colonies introduced paper money. But revenue collected from taxes often proved inadequate to meet budgetary requirements and insufficient to back up the notes. The value of paper money dropped drastically, notably in New England. In 1741 Parliament, concerned about creditors both in Britain and the colonies who faced losses, ended the operations of the Land Bank set up to issue paper money in Massachusetts. In 1751 all the New England colonies were forbidden to print money except in times of war or emergency. But when Virginia and North Carolina turned to paper money to ease the economic pinch of the costly French and Indian War, the British Board of Trade denounced the act as economic heresy and in 1764 further issuance of paper money was banned throughout the colonies.

Strangled by the need for currency and seriously short of credit, the colonial businessmen worked desperately to expand their commerce, particularly with the French and Spanish West Indies, which paid in cash. This often meant smuggling in open defiance of a law which imposed heavy duties on such commerce. But legality was not an impressive argument against the grim statistics on overseas trade. The excess of imports from England over exports rose from £50,680 in 1700 to an annual average of £755,000 between 1761 and 1770. The sterling gap was greatest in the northern colonies, but every province except Carolina, which benefited from heavy rice exports, had suffered from devastating trade imbalances in the decade before the American Revolution. The benefits to England of this legislated advantage were incalculable. "For let visionary writers say what they will," the Earl of Shelburne declared in the House of Lords in October 1775, "it is a plain and incontestable fact that the commerce of America is the vital stream of this great empire."

A colonial iron founder depended mostly on his own muscle power. The bellows for his furnace were pumped by water, but the molten iron was ladled by hand. In 1648 it was reported that the furnace at Saugus, Massachusetts, was producing "8 tun per weeke, and their barre iron is as good as Spanish."

Of all the occupations carried on by Europeans in the Western Hemisphere, fishing was the earliest. Only a few years after Columbus reached America, Dutch, Portuguese, English and French fishermen were at work off the Grand Banks of Newfoundland, and fishery operations have continued from that day on. In colonial times the best grade of fish went to the Catholic nations of southern Europe in return for salt and wine. The worst (candidly called "refuse") was sent to the West Indian sugar islands to feed the slaves. Until the end of the French and Indian War in 1763, the French competed with colonial and English fishermen for the cod of the Grand Banks. After France was defeated, English fishermen met fierce competition from the New Englanders and complained bitterly that the colonists were driving them out.

Whales were almost as useful in the colonial economy as yaks are to Tibetans. Whale oil was used in soapmaking and it lighted the lamps in houses and on the streets; spermaceti, a waxy solid, made the finest candles; bone from the whale's jaws was carved into corset stays and whip handles; ambergris, a fatty substance excreted by the sperm whale, was, and is, a fixative in making perfumes. When the sperm whale became the prime quarry, whalers roved farther, seeking their valuable prey up and down the stormy Atlantic as far north as Baffin Bay, as far south as the Falkland Islands. Nantucket, New Bedford, Mystic and Sag Harbor were the great centers of the industry.

The timber resources of the colonies were an incalculable source of wealth. A flourishing trade in lumber used in building served domestic and foreign

needs. In New England, white pine proved the mainstay of shipbuilding. Prize trees furnished masts, yards and spars for the Royal Navy, hard-pressed to get timber from the Baltic countries. Crown surveyors marked tall white pines over a certain girth with a broad arrow—to reserve them for the navy. But at the same time England obligingly offered an import bounty on American lumber and paid a premium for masts and spars. The white oak of the Middle Colonies was valuable both for barrels and ship timber. Other hard woods—walnut, cherry and red maple—supported the cabinetmaker's trade. Potash, extracted from wood ashes, was used by the textile industry. The naval stores industry of the South was based on the great stands of yellow pine and was promoted by liberal bounties offered by Parliament for American naval stores—tar, pitch, rosin and turpentine.

HOME furnishings and workshop crafts dominated the industrial activity. The output ranged from finely crafted furniture to rifles. Homespun, a family-produced cloth, was shipped and sold among the colonies. Enough felt hats made from beaver fur were being exported to Europe and the West Indies to prompt the severely restrictive Hat Act in 1732, in order to protect the British industry. Colonial hatters paid little attention to the law.

The iron industry of the Middle Colonies and the South was a notable exception to the usual American home workshop, with its family labor, a few journeymen and apprentices. Iron manufacture required large-scale investment in plant and equipment. Centered on the "iron plantations"—huge tracts organized into largely self-sufficient, quasi-feudal communities—the iron industry by 1775 kept more blast furnaces and forges busy than in England and Wales combined. Naturally, this had aroused unfavorable Parliamentary action. As early as 1750, the Iron Act had tried to encourage colonial production of pig and bar iron (which England then needed) and to suppress colonial competition in finished iron, steel, tools and hardware (which it did not).

Some colonial manufacturers and farmers found the Navigation Acts helpful. Shipbuilders and producers of things like naval stores or indigo welcomed them because the acts gave these products a favored position. But on the whole the laws were restrictive in their effect. As an instance, the forced routing of tobacco through Britain, instead of directly to the Continental markets, raised costs and sharply reduced sales. This was an artificial restraint on what should have been a natural growing trade, for by 1773 Britain consumed less than four million of the 100 million pounds of tobacco imported from America. The remainder was re-exported, mostly to Holland, France and Germany. Colonial textile makers, lumbermen and ironmasters also felt hobbled by the laws. It is highly significant that the greatest industrial expansion in the post-Revolutionary period occurred in precisely those industries—notably textiles and iron—which had been shackled by the Navigation Acts.

Despite currency shortages, adverse trade balances and the restraints imposed by Britain's navigation and trade laws, the rich economic potential of the colonies was unmistakably apparent by 1775. A prosperous and inventive labor force, a cheap and virtually limitless supply of land, a resourceful maritime enterprise were strong assets. Once the restraints of British mercantilism were lifted, that economy was bound to make enormous leaps forward and, in place of its former subordinate role, American commerce and industry would supply the solid base for the political structure of the emergent nation.

DOWN TO THE SEA:

COLONIAL FISHING

One of the earliest colonial industries, fishing has always been important to America. As fast as boats were built, crews were found, and villages such as Gloucester and Marblehead became centers for the growing fleets. The Grand Bank had long been a favorite of European fishermen, and colonists were soon fishing there, as well as at the Sable Island and St. Pierre Banks. The ports of Nantucket and New Bedford prospered as the colonial whaling industry expanded. By the outbreak of the Revolution, the American whaling fleet numbered well over 300 ships.

The confident fraternity of labor

AMERICANS in the 18th Century wholeheartedly agreed that labor was dignified and virtuous. Guided by the Protestant equation of diligent toil with godliness, the colonists applied themselves to every manner of trade, craft and agriculture. Every group, from slaves and indentured servants to the urban gentry, produced skilled craftsmen. In the years before 1775, one of the best examples of the self-made man was versatile Paul Revere, an American version of the Renaissance man. Silversmith, engraver, soldier and patriot, Revere's driving energy, ingenuity and diverse skills made him outstanding among a generation of farmers, fishermen and artisans who strove for the wealth and prominence an expanding economy made possible. From the shipbuilding industry of New England to the tobacco, indigo and rice plantations of the South, Americans formed a confident fraternity of labor. Households produced clothing (they supplied an estimated three fourths of all the textiles used in the colonies), furniture, tools, shoes, and other goods of wood, cloth and leather. Flour mills and factories boomed, farms and trades thrived, and exports expanded as the commercial foundation of the future was laid.

WORKADAY LIFE in the colonies is seen in an illustration of a maxim from Benjamin Franklin's *Almanack*. The carpentry, beekeeping and blacksmithing that are shown here dramatized such "Poor Richard" proverbs as "He that hath a trade hath an estate."

THE NEW REALISM in American painting is shown in this portrait of Paul Revere by John Singleton Copley, the first major painter of the colonies. Copley portrayed his friend around 1765, just as he saw him when he entered his shop. Copley's realistic style was an innovation and contrasted strongly with the formal classical mode of European painters of the day.

The waterfront of Philadelphia in 1720, when it was second only to Boston as the colonies' busiest commercial center, is shown in a painting

NEWFOUNDLAND'S FISHING INDUSTRY is explained in this drawing of around 1720. Each step in the processing of cod is shown, from catching (C), to extracting the oil (I), to drying the fish (M). By the end of the 16th Century, many European nations were exploiting these fishing grounds, and the Newfoundland fisheries employed some 200 ships and thousands of men.

by Peter Cooper. By 1769, Philadelphia's 28,000 people made it the largest city in the colonies, and one of the largest in the British Empire.

Shipbuilders, fishermen and traders to the world

As the colonies' rich harvests from farms, forests and seas multiplied during the 18th Century, the building of vessels needed to carry these products to trade centers on many seas grew in importance. Timber was abundant and within easy access of the shipyards which dotted both the inland streams and coastal towns. With a tradition dating back to 1607, when the 30-ton *Virginia* was launched on the Kennebec River, the skilled master builders and wrights of New England were ready for the orders that poured in during the golden age of shipbuilding between 1700 and 1735. And all down the coast, through the middle colonies, yards were producing schooners, sloops and small bay craft for intercolonial traffic. They also launched sturdy oceangoing barks for commerce throughout the Atlantic world.

In New England, the ships and ports of the booming fishing industry furnished employment for 10,000 men by 1765. So important was cod to the new nation's economy that John Adams, during the negotiations for the Treaty of Paris of 1783, fought for and won America's right to fish off the Newfoundland banks. Ships crammed with staples from Georgia, the Carolinas, Maryland and Virginia plied the rough transoceanic route to the mother country, returning with a variety of fabricated items, fine woolens and linen goods. A robust breed of Yankee sea captains voyaged to the West Indies and Africa, their ships laden with pork, dried fish, lumber, corn and rum, which they exchanged for sugar, molasses, ginger —and slaves. Despite English attempts to curtail commerce with French, Dutch and Spanish possessions, the colonies' foreign commerce on the eve of the revolution accounted for one seventh of the empire's total trade.

MARYLAND'S SHIPBUILDING is detailed in a mid-18th Century oil of Gray's Inn Creek shipyard near Chesapeake Bay by an anonymous artist. Shipyards lined the shores of colonial ports.

109

UNINHIBITED HIGH JINKS in Dutch Guiana give zest to John Greenwood's painting of the 1750s, "Sea Captains Carousing in Surinam." In such out-of-the-way places, Puritan restraint often succumbed to revels like the one above. Captain Nicholas Cooke (in profile, holding a pipe), a future governor of Rhode Island, is conversing quietly at the round table. The man with

cheek cupped in hand is thought to be Stephen Hopkins, a signer of the Declaration of Independence. Nearby, a sleeper gets a shower of grog from one captain and an unexpected pocketful from another, Captain Ambrose Page, himself in fiery peril. The distressed fellow at the doorway, who is every bit as sick as some of the others, may be a self-portrait of the artist.

A FARMER'S HOMESTEAD in the Catskill Mountains is recorded in this view of Marten Van Bergen's house in Leeds, New York. Dated about 1735, the mural was painted over his mantelpiece.

In prospering colonies a growing desire for beauty

BY the mid-1700s, the struggle for survival of early colonial days was fading into history, and the prospering Americans were no longer satisfied with primitive living arrangements. The simple, functional houses, with details dating back to the Middle Ages, showed a new elegance, reflecting, if not the leisure, the growing wealth of the colonists. While professional architects had not yet appeared, carpenters and gentlemen amateurs, influenced by classic designs, displayed a boldness of interpretation that went beyond the patterns in the European building manuals they consulted.

Fine household objects were also in wide demand. Crafted furniture was freely adapted from Dutch and English models. Many of today's treasured antiques, such as the Windsor chair, Queen Anne-style tables and chests, and a variety of everyday utensils like dinnerware and drinking mugs, evolved during this busy time. In the towns of the North the ambitious artisan achieved a significant status, fashioning everything from clocks to stoneware. He was, according to one sermon of the period, "a rare Example of Industry, a great Redeemer of his Time, taking care to spend not only his Days, but his Hours well, and giving Diligence in his Business. . . ."

A MINISTER'S HOME, built in 1683 at Topsfield, Massachusetts, is called the "Parson Capen House." This predecessor of the famous Cape Cod style was restored in 1913.

Indigo processing in South Carolina, stimulated by English demand for the blue dye, is shown in an 18th Century drawing. From harvesting

A TOBACCO WHARF in Virginia is seen in this drawing *(left)*, dated 1775. Hogsheads of the cured tobacco leaves are hammered shut and then loaded into oceangoing vessels which could easily reach as far as the private wharves of the Tidewater plantations.

A NEW METHOD for the harvesting of wheat in Maryland is shown in this illustration of 1788. Using this technology, which increased daily results by 160 per cent, each harvester had a specialized task, such as reaping, carrying bags or loading wagons.

An agricultural civilization based on rich soil

ALTHOUGH much progress was made toward establishing a business economy, the colonies had an essentially agrarian civilization throughout the 1700s. In 1760 ninety per cent of colonial America's 1,700,000 people relied on the soil for their living. In the South, especially, the favorable topography, rich soil, warm climate and ample rainfall of the Tidewater region, stretching from Maryland to Georgia, encouraged the widespread cultivation of profitable export staples.

By the end of the period, great tobacco, rice and indigo plantations produced a substantial part of the colonies' wealth. The resulting landed "aristocracy" dominated the social and political life of the region. Nevertheless, the plain fruit, grain and vegetable farmers, scattered from coastal lands to the back country, both South and North, were in the numerical majority. Their fertile holdings, which ranged from 50 to a few hundred acres, were cornucopialike in their profuse bounty. Employing time-honored methods, these farmers harvested a variety and quality of products rated among the finest in the world. A self-sufficient people, they grew the raw materials for their clothing, tanned hides for the family's shoes, hunted and fished for both eating and sale. It was still a time when few had luxuries, but almost all had the ingenuity to generate an abundance of life's necessities.

to pressing and drying, skilled slaves performed the varied tasks.

Newly emancipated farmers with varied skills

NEW ENGLAND'S soil was as obstinate as the South's was tractable, and its bitter winters yielded reluctantly to brief summers. Although the long cold seasons made possible remarkable fireside crafts like the wall tapestry shown below, climate and terrain combined to discourage large-scale agriculture. Yet many New England farmers raised enough for a spare and frugal but healthy life. In the middle Atlantic colonies the fertile valleys of New York, New Jersey and Pennsylvania produced an outpouring of fruits and vegetables. Vast yields were harvested in the wheat fields of these "bread colonies," while broad pastures produced hay to support a thriving livestock trade. Inventive, ambitious and free of his Old World peasant status, by 1750 the colonial farmer had become an independent, prideful landholder.

SKILLED NEEDLEWORK forms this fanciful illustration of Adam and Eve, embroidered on linen with twisted threads in 1760 by Mary Titcomb, a New England girl.

SELF-SUFFICIENT LIFE of the Moravians at Bethlehem, Pennsylvania, is seen in this 1757 picture. In 20 years, the wilderness had been replaced by rich, orderly farmland.

6. BUILDERS OF A NEW CULTURE

Bᴦ 1775 an American character and nationality were clearly emerging. The colonial subjects of George III in 1775 were entirely different from those who had planted Virginia and Plymouth 150 years earlier in James I's reign. The distance that separated them was as great as that which separated America from the Old World and its people, so long and so completely divided along tight linguistic, national and religious lines.

No one can measure precisely how much the special American traits came from the infusion of non-English elements into colonial life, and how much in response to the challenge of a new environment. Tom Paine, British-born, and J. Hector St. John Crèvecoeur, a French settler, both saw America as a melting pot, but later experts took a different view. For example, the American historian George Bancroft insisted that the Thirteen Colonies were basically English and that only one fifth of the American people had a language other than English as their mother tongue. His estimate appeared to be confirmed by a Census Bureau report of 1909 which served as the statistical basis for post-World War I laws that curtailed immigration from lands presumably not heavily represented in colonial America.

We now know that this report used a wrong approach. It drew its statistics from names in the census of 1790, but failed to consider that immigrant families usually Anglicized their names. Thus national origins can often be determined only with difficulty. The German *Roth*, for example, is inextricably

THE FRANKLIN HAND PRESS appears here with a page of the Boston journal for which Ben wrote at 16. Newspapers like this became a significant force in colonial America.

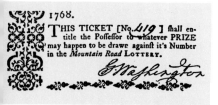

America's flourishing 18th Century lotteries built bridges, paved streets and financed colleges, hospitals, defenses and libraries. Even George Washington signed and sold some tickets (above) and managed raffles. The varied prizes included land, diamonds, telescopes, silverware and a Negro woman.

confused with variants of the British *Rhodes*, the German *Scherer* with the Scottish *Shearer*, the German *Kohler* with the British *Collier*. The Dutch *Van Kouwenhoven* became *Conover*; the gravestone of *Dirck Kuyper* reads *Richard Cooper*. Similar examples are abundant in every immigrant nationality.

It is now conservatively estimated that non-English immigrants made up some 40 per cent of the colonial population, though proportions varied from place to place. The Yankees of New England were about 70 per cent English, with a liberal infusion of Scots, Scotch-Irish, Celtic Irish, plus some French and Germans; in the South, English settlers comprised considerably less of the total. Pennsylvania was only about one third English.

The degree to which a group continues to speak its mother tongue is a useful, but by no means infallible, index of cultural durability. By that test the Dutch failed badly to resist the impact of the British. Even before the English occupation of 1664, some 18 different languages seem to have been spoken in New Amsterdam; later the Dutch could not hold their dikes against the floodwaters of assimilation that the English let loose. By 1762 the Dutch even invited a Presbyterian minister to preach in English at the Dutch Reformed Church of New York. Though English superseded Dutch, some traces of the language still remain in certain American words like *cruller, cooky, boss, crib, stoop* and *spook*. And though little survived of Dutch culture, proud family traditions are preserved by such renowned families as the Schuylers, the Roosevelts, the De Peysters and the Brevoorts.

The Germans were the largest non-English group in colonial America, and also the most tenacious of the minorities in clinging to their native cultural ties. Pennsylvania alone had 100,000 Germans by 1776, and many thousands more had settled on the frontiers of Maryland, Virginia and North Carolina. William Penn recruited many directly from the Continent. A sizable group of Germans led by Francis Daniel Pastorius responded to Penn's invitation and settled Germantown in 1683. These were followed a few years later by Pietists under Johann Kelpius. The greatest number of Germans came from the war-ravaged Rhineland. By 1709 some 13,000 destitute German Palatines had arrived in England. But England was only a temporary stopping place, and nearly half of them went on to New York, North Carolina and Pennsylvania.

The first wave of German immigrants brought mostly German Quakers; Mennonites; Baptist Brethren, or Dunkers; and other small sects who made Lancaster County their own. A second wave after 1730 consisted largely of Lutherans and Calvinists. Still a third group called the United Brethren, or

Moravians, had originally fled from Moravia in Austria. They established themselves in the Pennsylvania towns of Bethlehem, Nazareth and Lititz, and at Salem, North Carolina. These groups won recognition for their communal industrial projects, their fine schools, their magnificent choral music and their missionary work among the Indians.

Most German immigrants were poor, and families were often broken up by purchasers of their indentures. But through thrift and industry, prudent farm management and skills in the crafts, they overcame initial handicaps and achieved comfort and independence. Their gunsmiths pioneered the Pennsylvania (or Kentucky) rifle, their wagonmakers the Conestoga wagon.

In the area between the Lehigh and the Susquehanna, the Germans formed a cultural island cut off from the mainstream of the English-speaking population. With their own printing presses, newspapers, schools, churches and language (a corruption of German and English popularly called Pennsylvania Dutch), they posed a problem to Pennsylvania's leaders and molders of public opinion. As broadminded as Benjamin Franklin was, he felt concern about this self-imposed isolation, and feared that unless the current of German immigrants could be diverted to other colonies, they would "soon so outnumber us that all the advantages we have will, in my opinion, be not able to preserve our language." Jefferson, too, wished the Germans would distribute themselves among the native-born for "quicker amalgamation."

In the 17th Century the Scots formed a separate nation connected with England only because the two peoples shared the same monarch. Varying English dialects were spoken in the Lowlands; the Highlanders brought their Gaelic to America. Most of the emigrant Scots were Presbyterian Lowlanders who had settled in northern Ireland when James I began his "Great Plantation" to put down rebellion among chieftains in the Ulster area. Persecuted by Cromwell, and later by William and Mary after the battle of the Boyne, the native Irish were relegated to the backward mountainous regions with the poorest, least arable land.

The Scotch-Irish, as the Ulster Scots came to be known, fared only little better than the supplanted Irish. They were hard hit by the Woolen Act of 1699, which made it illegal for their weavers to export their cloth to any foreign country. Furthermore, an act of 1704 disenfranchised all who would not conform to the established Anglican Church. Disillusioned and embittered, a steady stream embarked for America; some 200,000 Scots had left Ulster up to 1776. A substantial number of the Scotch-Irish settled in the back country

Philadelphia's newly built "Bettering House" (far left) sheltered and gave work to the city's indigent. The Pennsylvania Hospital, not to be completed until 1805, is seen at the right of this 1767 print. The existence of both institutions by the mid-18th Century sharply deflated the earlier boast that "no one need ever starve or be in want in this fruitful country."

of Pennsylvania. Many moved down the Appalachian valleys into the Carolinas, where they settled the frontier wilderness, often as squatters, and took over a considerable share of the Indian trade.

Highlanders began coming to America after the unsuccessful Scottish rebellions of 1715 and 1745-1746, which attempted to restore the Stuarts to the English throne. Some came as fugitives, most as exiles who swore allegiance to the Hanoverian kings of England as the price of their freedom. Most Highlanders gravitated to communities made up of their countrymen on the farming frontier. Many Lowlanders, pressed by rising unemployment in Scotland, emigrated to new homes up and down the Atlantic Seaboard. When England and Scotland were joined by the Act of Union of 1707, Scottish businessmen at last had the full benefits of the English trade laws, and many of them emigrated to the colonies, where they became important in the tobacco trade of Maryland and Virginia. During the Revolution most of the Scots remained loyal to the crown. The Scotch-Irish, on the contrary, stood in the forefront of rebellion, for they, along with the Celtic Irish, abhorred English rule. An inscription on a tombstone in Virginia's Shenandoah Valley dramatically epitomizes the history of these emigrants: "Here lie the remains of John Lewis, who slew the Irish lord, settled Augusta County, located the town of Staunton, and furnished five sons to fight the battles of the American Revolution."

Grave of mien, Jonathan Edwards, the New England theologian and revivalist, had a logical mind but a hopelessly delicate constitution, and he died at 54 of a fever following a smallpox inoculation, at the pinnacle of his career. One of the 70 rigorous resolutions he set for himself was "never to do anything which I should be afraid to do if it were the last hour of my life."

IN 16th Century France, relations between the Huguenots, as John Calvin's French followers were known, and the Catholics grew steadily worse. Thousands of Huguenots were killed in one night during the St. Bartholomew's Massacre of 1572. Many of the survivors found refuge in England and Holland, and their descendants often emigrated to the New World. In 1598 Henri IV promulgated the Edict of Nantes, which granted the Huguenots toleration. Decades of relative peace followed, but when the edict was revoked in 1685, many more Huguenots fled to the English colonies, the bulk of them going to South Carolina, Virginia, New York and Pennsylvania. Names like Huger, Izard, Laurens and Porcher in South Carolina; Girard, Boudinot and Roberdeau in Philadelphia; DeLancey, Jay and Delano (from de La Noye) in New York; and Faneuil, Revere and Bowdoin in New England supply ample evidence of the wide political and social prominence achieved by the Huguenots on the eve of the Revolution.

A relatively small group (about 50,000 in 1776), the French assimilated remarkably well. In South Carolina many became Anglicans; in Pennsylvania, they mingled with the Swiss and Germans; in New York, with the Dutch and English. For example, John Jay, first Chief Justice of the United States, was the grandson of Augustus Jay, a French Huguenot exile who settled in New York about 1686. His mother was a Dutch Van Cortlandt, and he himself married the youngest daughter of William Livingston, governor of New Jersey during the Revolution, thus combining French, Dutch and Scottish stock. Other Huguenot families had similar stories. With their great drive, intelligence and ingenuity, the French left a distinctive mark on American culture.

No single religious denomination was ever able to control all Thirteen Colonies. Although predominantly Protestant, the religious groups remained fragmented. Of 2.5 million Americans in 1776 no more than one fifth were Church of England; at least double that number belonged to various Calvinist denominations (New England Puritans or Congregationalists, Presbyterians, Dutch

and German Reformed Churches). Other colonists were Quakers, Lutherans, Pietists, Baptists and Methodists, and there were, in addition, approximately 25,000 Roman Catholics and 2,000 Jews.

Most of the transplanted Protestant sects had sought religious independence for themselves rather than toleration for others, and although ideas of religious toleration were known to Milton's England and to Roger Williams' America, it took another century for their fruition. To safeguard their religious independence, groups like the Anglicans and the Puritans felt it essential to be sustained, or "established," by the state, with the salary of the minister and other church expenses paid by taxing all the people regardless of affiliation.

In the mother country the Church of England had long enjoyed establishment, but by 1700 the Anglican Church had secured this privileged position only in the colonies of Maryland and Virginia. Elsewhere, there were but a few scattered Anglican churches in Charleston, Philadelphia, New York and Boston. But in 1701, when the Society for the Propagation of the Gospel in Foreign Parts, known as the S.P.G., was set up, the fortunes of the Church of England improved. Founded to convert Indians and Negroes and to bolster Anglicanism where it was shaky, the S.P.G. made some headway, notably in South Carolina. It was handicapped, however, by the low prestige and lower caliber of the Anglican clergy, too often curates from England in whom the faith burned dimly. Since the Bishop of London controlled the American Anglicans, it was impossible to recruit a native ministry of dedicated men. Only a bishop could ordain priests, and with no bishop in America, colonials had to go to England for ordination, a journey few could afford. Some Anglicans felt that the obvious solution was to have a bishop in America who would not only ordain native ministers but hold a tighter rein on church discipline. This proposal drew crossfire: Puritans and other dissenters in the northern colonies feared an increase of the Anglican establishment and viewed bishops as smacking of popery; Virginia planters, long accustomed to naming and dismissing their own pastors, were unwilling to surrender this power. The Revolution settled the question by ending all fears about an established church, and this weakened the opposition to naming bishops. The first American bishop, named by the church in 1783, was—ironically enough—Samuel Seabury of Connecticut, who had been a militant Tory.

Itinerant preacher George Whitefield, who made seven visits to America, rose from the rowdy atmosphere of an English tavern to become the most eloquent man of his day. But many English and colonial divines were enraged by his arrogant, egotistical evangelism, in the course of which he once contemptuously called clerics "slothful shepherds and dumb dogs."

I N 1765 an Anglican official in Charleston reported: "The principles of most of the colonists in America are independent in matters of religion, as well as republican in those of government." By this date, most denominations, even the aristocratic Anglican, showed a very considerable degree of democracy, with local congregations exercising control over their churches. Such congregational control had always been characteristic of Massachusetts' Puritan churches. Paradoxically, this home-rule system made the austere Puritan churches bastions of intolerant orthodoxy that yielded only slowly to the tides of heterodoxy and rationalism. But no church can long maintain its pioneer fervor, and by the 1660s the Puritan elders had to make concessions to less zealous men and women among their parishioners. First they admitted to baptism children of baptized persons, even though the parents had not themselves experienced the religious conversion required for "election," or full membership. This Half-Way Covenant, as it was called, erased most distinctions between the "elect" and all others. Then, in 1699, Boston's Brattle Street

123

Church was the first to allow communion without a public confession of faith.

Other blows shook the very foundations of unreconstructed Puritanism. The role that church leaders played in the notorious Salem witchcraft trials damaged their prestige. The old guard headed by Increase and Cotton Mather, to reassert control, tried to unite the Congregational churches in Massachusetts under a governing body of ministers, in imitation of the Presbyterian system. But an outspoken liberal, John Wise, pastor of Ipswich, blasted these efforts in 1717 with an essay ("Wise's cursed libel," Cotton Mather called it) in which he argued that a communicant should have a voice in the administration of his church similar to the right of a citizen in relation to his government. In trenchant phrases Wise transformed the Puritan concept of the Bible commonwealth into a philosophy of democratic and egalitarian government limited by law. This pre-Revolutionary democratic thinking of Wise shook up the Puritan oligarchy, and a steady drift toward rationalism undermined it further. More and more Puritans accepted the fashionable Arminianism of the Anglicans, a doctrine arguing for a greater degree of free will than Calvin's predestinarianism. Later the Puritan dogma was further diluted by a generous infusion of the tenets of deism and Unitarianism.

The orthodox Puritans were hit from still another direction by the evangelical fervor called the Great Awakening that swept the colonies in the 1730s. A hellfire-and-brimstone revolt against rationalism, this revival movement had as its most potent single influence the eloquent English evangelist George Whitefield, a friend of the Methodist leader John Wesley. In his various trips to America between 1738 and 1770, Whitefield preached from Massachusetts to Georgia, drawing enormous crowds. From his pulpit in Northampton, Massachusetts, meanwhile, Jonathan Edwards expounded doctrines that gave the Great Awakening a more philosophic expression. Edwards used his cutting logic to combat what he called the "fashionable new divinity" of the liberal-thinking rationalists. Moreover, he captured in striking and lurid phrases the apocalyptic spirit of the revival.

Many were roused by the evangelical appeal, but others were repelled by the shrieks, shakes and swoonings of the enraptured congregations. Samuel Johnson of Connecticut, for example, sought the peaceful order of the Church of England, and preached the idealistic doctrines of Bishop George Berkeley. In Boston, Jonathan Mayhew preached Puritanism as a rational and practical system, rejecting the Trinitarian view and affirming the doctrine of free will. Speaking out boldly as the Revolution neared, Mayhew defended the people's right to disobey a government acting contrary to God's laws and fired his Puritan listeners with righteous republican zeal.

In its long history since 1693, the College of William and Mary in Virginia has housed armies as well as students. During the Yorktown campaign, the entire campus, including the building (above) designed by Christopher Wren, was occupied first by the forces of Cornwallis and then by French troops. Later, the college lodged Confederate and Union armies.

T HE 18th Century was marked by the philosophical movement called the Enlightenment, a rationalistic and scientific approach to life. Benjamin Franklin perhaps best exemplified this school in America. His volume on electricity was to be the most influential American book of colonial times. But education as a whole lagged far behind such outstanding achievements. A Puritan innovation, American education reflected the Protestant Reformation, and religion and the classics dominated the curriculum at all levels.

The Puritans were first in education partly because they were better educated than most 17th Century pioneers. At least 130 university alumni came to New England before 1646, an average of one to every 40 or 50 families, an

astonishing proportion for that time. These alumni of Oxford and Cambridge Universities founded the Boston Latin School in 1635 and a college in 1636. (Two years later the college was named for a benefactor, John Harvard.) Then they forced the passage of the great Massachusetts school laws of 1642 and 1647. The 1642 act set fines for parents who failed to teach their children how to read. By the act of 1647 every town of 50 families was required to appoint a schoolteacher, and towns of 100 families had to set up a grammar school where children could be educated for Harvard.

IN the Middle Colonies, by contrast, education was largely a church effort. The outstanding New York schools were the Collegiate School, founded in 1638 under Dutch Reformed auspices but supported by the town of New Amsterdam, and Trinity School, founded in 1710 by the S.P.G. In Philadelphia the Friends' Public School, later known as William Penn Charter School, was established in 1689. In the South, the isolation of the plantations made the assembling of children in a formal schoolroom both expensive and impractical. So there was tutoring for the sons of the rich, apprenticeship for working-class children and pauper schools for the indigent. By 1775, however, private fee-supported schools and academies were taking hold.

Colonial colleges, with a few exceptions, pursued theological ends with a sectarian bias. The first, Harvard, was founded to make sure that the Puritans would be ministered to by literate preachers. The same purpose prompted a college in Connecticut in 1701, later named for its benefactor, Elihu Yale. In 1693 William and Mary was established in Virginia under Anglican auspices as "a seminary of ministers of the Gospel." The Great Awakening inspired a rash of others. Each sect hastened to found its own college, the New Side Presbyterians establishing Princeton in 1746; the Baptists, Brown in 1764 (but with no religious test for admission); the Dutch Reformed revivalists, Queen's College, or Rutgers, in 1766. In 1770 a Congregational minister, the Reverend Eleazar Wheelock, transformed an Indian missionary school begun earlier in Connecticut into Dartmouth College at Hanover, New Hampshire.

At least two institutions reflected new nondenominational influences. Franklin's Academy (later to become the University of Pennsylvania) was nonsectarian at the start. Soon, however, it came under Anglican direction. King's College (now Columbia) was initially sponsored by the Church of England, but an effort was made to conciliate the Presbyterian opposition by placing ministers of four other denominations on the first governing board. These two colleges also differed from the others in the courses they offered. Franklin, with his utilitarian outlook, emphasized the teaching of science and modern languages, and put less stress upon the classics. Samuel Johnson, first president of King's College, optimistically announced that the college would give instruction in "everything that can contribute to the true happiness" of youth, "both here and hereafter."

Despite their lofty ambitions the colleges did a good deal less than might have been expected to encourage the theoretical and experimental sciences. Nor did the colonial scientists enjoy the support of philanthropy. But scientists of the day found ample challenge in the still largely undiscovered and untapped resources of a vast continent which remained to be explored, mapped, described and botanized. William Byrd II explored western Virginia and North Carolina, and his racy narrative of a mixed Indian-and-poor-white frontier

Elihu Yale was "Born in America, in Europe bred, / In Africa travell'd, and in Asia wed, / Where long he liv'd and thriv'd; in London dead." A writer, official in India and diamond merchant, he donated three bales of goods, some books and a portrait of George I, worth in all £800, to a college in New Haven. The school took his name and, in exchange, he received lasting fame.

Puritan clergyman Cotton Math-er was a curious blend of religious zealot and calm scientist. A dedi-cated student of sorcery, he helped, through his writings, to set off the Salem witch hunt of 1692. But his good works won him popular es-teem, and his numerous books on physics, biology, astronomy and medicine led to his election as a Fellow of England's Royal Society.

life has become a classic of its kind. Young George Washington, who pene-trated deep into the Ohio country, added much to geographical lore.

Botany flourished. John Clayton gathered an enormous fund of data in Vir-ginia; John Bartram, a Quaker farmer, collected exotic specimens on his ex-tensive travels and set up his own botanical garden near Philadelphia. Mark Catesby wrote the most extensive work on the natural history of the South. Cotton Mather, whose mind was both prejudiced and experimental, contribut-ed a series of letters on natural history and biology to the *Philosophical Trans-actions* of England's renowned Royal Society. In 1721 Mather also wrote the first lengthy colonial commentary on Newton's *Principia Mathematica*, thus ac-quainting America with the law of gravitation.

Other men were also pursuing the physical sciences. Cadwallader Colden supplemented Newton's ideas with the highly original theory that gravitation was a force exerted by an elastic, contractive form of matter. Harvard profes-sor John Winthrop IV, whose ancestors included governors and scientists, made early observations on the nature of sunspots and planetary movements, and sponsored an expedition to Newfoundland in 1761 to observe the passage of Venus across the sun. In Philadelphia ingenious David Rittenhouse con-structed clocks, mathematical instruments and an orrery, a working model of the solar system. And Benjamin Franklin, that most versatile of all American colonials, achieved the status of an international celebrity with his contribu-tions to both theoretical science and invention.

For pioneers, the colonists were a remarkably bookish people. They brought with them or imported from Europe books on theology, science, the classics, outlines of universal knowledge and a few lawbooks. Remarkable collections were assembled by men like John Winthrop Jr., who in the late 17th Century boasted the largest scientific library in America. Those who could not buy their own books often could borrow them. In the 18th Century the S.P.G. started libraries for public use in the South. Franklin established a subscrip-tion library in Philadelphia; others were begun at Newport, Charleston, New York and elsewhere. Later Franklin observed that libraries had "improved the general conversation of Americans, made the common tradesman and farmers as intelligent as most gentlemen from other countries, and perhaps have con-tributed in some degree to the stand so generally made throughout the colo-nies in defense of their privileges."

STARTING with the *Bay Psalm Book* of 1640, colonial publishing flourished. Chronicles, histories and travel accounts; bestsellers like *The Day of Doom* by Michael Wigglesworth, whose ballad stanzas made children shiver at the prospect of death and damnation; Mary Rowlandson's gripping narrative of her captivity among the Indians; all testified to America's thirst for reading. The *New England Primer*, combining the ABCs with a hard core of religious matter, became a stand-by whose sales ultimately ran into the millions. In the 18th Century, almanacs by Nathaniel Ames and Ben Franklin were household necessities, and a Revolutionary generation was soon to argue the merits of political tracts by James Otis, John Dickinson and Tom Paine.

It took half a century after the first printing press for newspapers to make their appearance, but newspapers were something of a novelty then, even in Europe. Though the public was avid for news, government officials were ex-tremely touchy and reacted violently to criticism. Printers who ventured to

tell the whole truth faced loss of business, revocation of their licenses and even jail sentences. Benjamin Harris had been imprisoned in Britain for criticizing the king. In Boston his *Publick Occurrences*, the colonies' first newspaper, was suppressed four days after its initial appearance in 1690 for daring to report that the English armed forces had allied themselves with "miserable savages." When James Franklin, editor of the *New-England Courant*, was jailed in 1722 for attacking the colonial government, he had his half brother Ben, then only 16, carry on the enterprise.

S EVENTEENTH Century newspapers needed a license from the crown, so a free press was impossible in England. When licensing was abandoned in 1695, censorship by the king's courts continued. Colonial authorities awarded government printing contracts to loyal printers and withheld them from their critics. Fearing this type of pressure, the elder William Bradford followed an almost obsequious policy when he established New York's first newspaper, the *Gazette*, in 1725. Bradford's former apprentice, a German immigrant named John Peter Zenger, took a different tack when he started a new paper with the backing of Lewis Morris, ousted Chief Justice of New York, and two prominent attorneys, James Alexander and William Smith. The very first issue of the *New-York Weekly Journal* in 1733 struck an independent, even belligerent note in colonial journalism. With grim, devastating humor, the *Journal* tore into the highhanded administration of Governor William Cosby. The governor was not amused. He threw Zenger into jail. At his arraignment in April 1735 for seditious libel, Zenger's backers, Alexander and Smith, served as counsel and challenged the judges' authority. The lawyers were promptly disbarred, but Zenger's friends induced an eminent trial lawyer, Andrew Hamilton of Philadelphia, to take over the case.

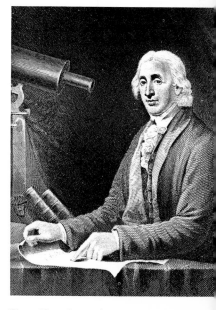

With an audacity matched by a rare eloquence, Hamilton went over the heads of the hostile judges and appealed to the jury to decide whether there was any basis in fact for Zenger's accusations that the governor had acted in violation of political and civil liberties. In memorable words Hamilton pointed out that this was "not the cause of a poor printer, nor of New York alone," and its consequences might "affect every freeman that lives under a British government on the main of America." He demanded a verdict in behalf of "the liberty—both of exposing and opposing arbitrary power (in these parts of the world, at least) by speaking and writing truth." The jury's "not guilty" finding aroused enormous interest both in the colonies and in Britain, where the courts had only recently ruled that truth was no defense in seditious libel. A popular couplet cheered:

> While free from force the press remains,
> Virtue and freedom chear our plains.

Despite the Zenger decision, newspapermen remained subject to various restraints, and the royal government's crude efforts to keep editors from presenting the facts to the people earned the undying enmity of many colonial printers. Of the 37 newspapers published in the colonies on the eve of the Revolution, 23 were patriot, only seven Loyalist, and seven neutral.

Along with letters and the press, the arts, crafts and architecture of the American colonies, each in its way, carried an original and authentic American style. Starting from designs imported from England and the Continent, the

The self-taught mathematician, astronomer and instrument-maker, David Rittenhouse, built America's first telescope but he never found a cure for "a constant heat in the pit of the stomach, affecting a space not exceeding the size of half a guinea. . . ." The ailment which humbled this great patriot and close friend of Franklin and Jefferson is today known as ulcers.

colonial craftsman changed, modified and invented to adapt his products to colonial uses and impart to them a local flavor.

Thus it is correct to speak of Philadelphia Chippendale because the local cabinetmakers put their own distinctive stamp on the basic designs of the London masters. The early art of the limners, who got their start painting houses, carriages and signs, and of the gravestone cutters, dedicated to symbols of death and resurrection, laid the foundations for an American art style, crude perhaps, but strikingly refreshing in its simplicity and originality. The self-taught portraiture of Robert Feke of Newport and the bourgeois realism of Maryland's Charles Willson Peale and Boston's John Singleton Copley (before he became captive to the more sophisticated manner of British painting) expressed the new civilization that was emerging in America. Though the affluent colonist might pore over English books of architecture by men like James Gibbs or Inigo Jones, and the churches in the colonies might bear the unmistakable stamp of the great Christopher Wren, the Georgian architecture that was transplanted to the colonies was as American as it was English. Nassau Hall in Princeton, with its simple cupola, may have followed established English design, but it belongs to the Delaware River country in the same sense that the magnificent Georgian-style Annapolis dwellings of architect William Buckland were typical of Maryland and the Georgian homes of Charleston were in fact a fine blend of English, West Indian and Huguenot motifs. The impulse was indubitably British, the execution peculiarly American.

EDMUND BURKE shrewdly observed that the "untractable spirit" of the colonists, their devotion to "liberty according to English ideas and on English principles," drew vital support from the widespread study of the law. Looking back at the early legal beginnings of the colonies, it seems a minor miracle that the common law of England and the legal profession should both have attained such eminence by 1776. Law was first administered in the colonies largely without benefit of lawyers, who were looked on with a distaste characteristic of frontier societies. The clergy in New England pressed hard for rule by Biblical law. The average settler wanted the kind of law and procedure which he had known in England—the local and customary law of borough and county courts, which was far less formal than the king's (or common) law administered in the royal courts of Westminster. Lacking trained lawyers, the colonists worked out legal systems which freed them from the rigid technicalities of medieval jurisprudence. Many archaisms of the procedural law and rules of evidence in England were abandoned; legal remedies were simplified. Real property in New England descended to all children rather than to the eldest son alone, and in the administration of estates, the old distinctions between real and personal property were abandoned. Criminal punishments were humanized, for in America people were too valuable to be put to death for small thefts as they were in England. Under Calvinist influence, a liberal civil divorce law was instituted in the Puritan colonies and married women enjoyed various legal rights denied them in England.

Many of these radical reforms did not survive the conservative reaction that set in around 1700. By then the royal government could curb an independent legal policy through devices such as its veto on colonial laws or the review by the king in council of decisions rendered by colonial courts. And the rising propertied and merchant classes pressed for the adoption of England's legal

THE
TENTH MUSE
Lately fprung up in AMERICA.
OR
Severall Poems, compiled with great variety of Wit and Learning, full of delight.
Wherein efpecially is contained a compleat difcourfe and defcription of
The Four {Elements, Conftitutions, Ages of Man, Seafons of the Year.
Together with an Exact Epitomie of the Four Monarchies, viz.
The {Affyrian, Perfian, Grecian, Roman.
Alfo a Dialogue between Old England and New, concerning the late troubles.
With divers other pleafant and ferious Poems.
By a Gentlewoman in thofe parts.
Printed at London for Stephen Bowtell at the figne of the Bible in Popes Head-Alley. 1650.

Plays were often considered frivolous among the Puritans, but the publication of poetry was taken quite seriously. Anne Bradstreet, the anonymous "Gentlewoman" of the title page seen above, was the first professional poet in New England. One of the earliest American playbills still existing (below) was for a performance for charity of a comedy by William Congreve.

For the Benefit of the Poor.
Thursday, December 20, 1753.
At the New Theatre in Naffau-Street.
This Evening, will be prefented,
(Being the laft Time of performing till the Holidays,)
A COMEDY, called,
LOVE for LOVE:

End of Act 1ft, Singing by Mr. Adcock.
End of Act 2d, Singing by Mrs. Love.
In Act 3d, a Hornpipe by Mr Hulett
End of Act 4th, a Cantata by Mrs. Love.

To which will be added, a Ballad Farce, called,
FLORA, or, Hob in the Well.

Prices: BOX, 6s. PIT. 4s. GALLERY, 2s.
No Perfons whatever to be admitted behind the Scenes.

Play bill from the first theatre in New York in Nassau Street.

system, which they felt offered greater security to property and business.

The legal profession played a significant role in abetting this conservatism. Young men served their apprenticeship as clerks with established lawyers or attended London's Inns of Court, where barristers had been trained for centuries. To protect their monopolistic position and keep out pettifoggers ("the dirty dabblers of the law," John Adams called them), lawyers formed bar associations, and the courts set rigid standards for admission to practice. With the lawyer's advance in stature went wider political influence. Thomas Hutchinson, Tory governor of Massachusetts as well as chief justice, wryly observed: "I do not recollect that the town of Boston ever chose a lawyer to represent it under the second charter, until the year 1738." After that time, Hutchinson pointed out, lawyers had "taken the lead, and been much employed in the publick measures of this, and of the other colonies." When the Declaration of Independence was signed, 25 of its 56 signers belonged to the bar.

By the mid-18th Century, the English legal system was widely adopted. Lawyers now seemed to take malevolent delight in confounding courts, still chiefly composed of laymen, with technical distinctions and wrangles over trivialities. Rights and duties were often based on hairsplitting. The humanizing forces in the early colonial criminal law were counteracted by increases in the penalties for crimes against property, emulating the harsh English statutes. But, while it aided conservative property interests, the common law also gave the patriot lawyers (many lawyers chose to remain loyal to the crown) precedents for preserving the historic "rights of Englishmen."

In 1774 the Continental Congress based the right of the colonists to oppose excesses by Parliament on three foundation stones: "the immutable laws of nature, the principles of the English constitution and the several charters or compacts." The law of nature had profoundly shaped the colonies' substantive law in the 1600s, while the scriptural basis of the law of nature, though no longer as important as formerly, was not abandoned. Revolutionary political thought was still linked with theology. Even John Locke and other "social contract" writers, whose ideas formed the basis of so much Revolutionary political thinking, were, in a sense, expanding on the political Calvinism that had molded earlier New England thought. But the appeal to the "rights of Englishmen" was far more influential in the Revolutionary era than that to the "rights of man," and as a result common-law traditions were nurtured that have continued to flourish in our legal system.

The French-born essayist Hector St. John Crèvecoeur declared that "there is room for everybody in America," a land he referred to as "this smiling country." His faith remained unshaken, even after he returned from France in 1783 to discover that his home in upstate New York had been burned, his wife had died and his children had disappeared after an Indian raid.

JARED ELIOT, author of a colonial book on husbandry, remarked of the colonists "that in a sort, they began the world anew." As early as 1767 Benjamin Franklin predicted that America must become "a great country." Crèvecoeur saw the American as a man who left behind his "ancient prejudices" and discarded Europe's "mechanism of subordination."

All three paid tribute to the distinctive and the original in American life, to the rising spirit of nationalism as it was reflected in America's arts and letters, religious outlook and laws, cosmopolitan population and growing psychological unity. All three observers managed to capture in their writings something of the essence of this new breed of men who were meeting the challenge of the New World with new ideas and a new way of life, freed from the dead, restraining hand of the past and encouraged by the growing opportunities for cultural fulfillment. Now this new breed confronted a critical decade.

America's first citizen of the world

THE best-known man in the colonies was Benjamin Franklin of Philadelphia, who was a runaway printer's apprentice—and thus a lawbreaker—at the age of 17, a newspaper owner when he was 24 and a rich (and retired) commercial printer by the time he was 42. Then, in his second 42 years, he enhanced his reputation as a scientist, inventor, politician, philanthropist, diplomat, best-selling author, expert musician and favorite—when past 70—of some of the most charming ladies of sophisticated French society.

Franklin was born in 1706 in Boston. His father, who made candles and soap, sent the boy to school for only two years, but Franklin never stopped educating himself. When he fled his brother's printing shop, he had learned enough to work as a journeyman printer in London and then to set up his own shop in busy, Quaker-dominated Philadelphia. But his real interests were science and public affairs. He began trying to unite the colonies long before independence was thought of, and in his ripe old age he became a militant revolutionist. His greatest achievement was in proving, by his own life and example, that a man humbly born in colonial America could become the equal of anyone, anywhere.

A POPULAR COLONEL of the Philadelphia militia, Franklin *(center, opposite)* is honored at a 1756 parade. The year before, during repeated Indian attacks, he served on the Pennsylvania frontier.

PROFITABLE PRODUCTS of Franklin's press surround his bust *(above)* in the Yale Library. The *Poor Richard* almanac contains his maxim, "Have you somewhat to do to-morrow; do it to-day."

131

Franklin is shown at the center of "The Congress Voting Independence," an 18th Century work. "We must indeed all hang together, or

THE EARLIEST PORTRAIT of Franklin *(below)* shows him about 1748, the year he retired from business. He was already postmaster of Philadelphia and printer of the province of Pennsylvania.

Tireless public servant, sage advocate of defense

FRANKLIN'S brain teemed with ideas for improving his city, his country and himself. His great talent for persuading people to work hard, and work together, made most of his projects come true. He led in giving Philadelphia its first paved streets, first fire company and first regular police. He helped to make his adopted city the home of the first American lending library and the first learned society, the first public hospital and the first fire insurance company. He also founded the academy that grew into the modern University of Pennsylvania.

While helping his "dear Philadelphia" become the pre-

most assuredly we shall hang separately," he joked at this event.

A HARD-WORKING AGENT for colonial interests, Franklin is pictured here in 1767, soon after leading the long, successful fight to repeal the Stamp Act, which had so infuriated the Americans.

eminent city of the colonies, Franklin made sure of its safety from Indian attacks—by organizing militia, building forts and persuading the governor of New York (after a "great drinking of Madeira wine") to lend the Philadelphians 18 "fine cannon." He had to fight political battles against the pacifist Quakers and also against the Penn family in England, the nominal rulers of Pennsylvania, who opposed any defense measures that might cost them money. In 1754, at a meeting of seven colonies in Albany, Franklin presented his boldest scheme: a permanent council of defense, with a governor-general appointed by the king, to manage the military and frontier affairs of all the American colonies. The plan was ahead of its time; every colony either rejected or ignored it. Twenty-two years later, meeting with George III's guns at their heads *(painting above)*, they finally agreed to unite—and Franklin was there to give his wise counsel.

FIREMAN FRANKLIN, in a copy of an early painting, wears the emblem of the company he founded in 1736. Members ran to fires with buckets, carrying bags to pack rescued goods.

133

A DARING RESEARCHER, Franklin *(opposite)* snatches lightning with his kite. This painting, complete with cherubim, is by Benjamin West. The actual experiment took place in a Philadelphia field, with Franklin's son his only helper.

FRANKLIN'S STOVE is an iron box with side openings that burns less wood and spreads heat more efficiently than ordinary fireplaces. Designed in 1740, it was Franklin's first famous invention.

TWO-FACED CLOCK conceived in 1758 by Franklin shows hours and minutes *(bottom dial)* and seconds *(top)*. But it never became popular because it was so difficult to tell the hour at a glance.

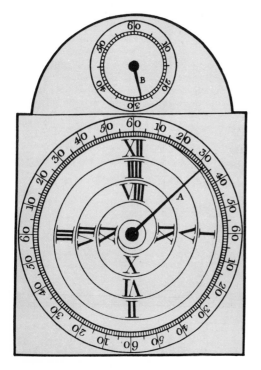

Master of the lightning

THE most dramatic incident in Franklin's life occurred in 1752 when he flew a silk kite into a thunderstorm and conducted lightning to earth by means of his own knuckles and body. If the lightning bolt had been more severe, he certainly would have been killed. As it turned out, the hazardous experiment was unnecessary; earlier that summer, unknown to Franklin, a Frenchman, using Franklin's idea of an iron pole on a tower, had demonstrated that lightning was a form of electricity. In his practical way, Franklin passed on, in his 1753 *Poor Richard* almanac, a way to use this knowledge: "Provide a small Iron Rod . . . one End being three or four Feet in the moist Ground, the other may be six or eight Feet above the highest Part of the Building. . . . A House thus furnish'd will not be damag'd by Lightning. . . ."

The lightning rod was only one of Franklin's many useful inventions. But his enduring prestige as a scientist was based on his far more important achievements in fundamental research. Beginning in 1747, in a series of patient experiments, he developed the theory that electricity was a single fluid and named "positive" and "negative" states of electricity, beginning the terminology which is still used today. To Franklin all knowledge was valuable, whether it had an immediate purpose or not. Once, as he watched a balloon ascension in Paris, someone asked him of what possible use this new toy could be. "What good," replied Franklin, "is a newborn baby?"

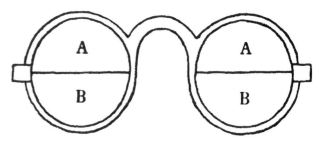

BIFOCAL SPECTACLES, another Franklin invention, are illustrated by his own diagram. To aid his 77-year-old eyes, he combined lenses for distant vision (A) with those for close-up reading (B).

A WIDE RANGE OF INTERESTS attracted Franklin's ever-questing mind. This still-life photograph illustrates some of them. The background is an early French edition of his map of the Gulf Stream, the first dependable one ever published. It was based partly on data he obtained from his mother's family, the whaling Folgers of Nantucket, and partly on his own observations during several ocean crossings. The other objects, beginning at lower left and proceeding clockwise around the picture, are rhubarb, which he introduced to Philadelphia from England; a pigeon, like those he raised to study environmental effects on birds; silkworm cocoons and mulberry leaves, which he urged Americans to cultivate; an American cardinal, which he proposed that Europeans

import for its beauty; whirlwinds, waterspouts and the aurora borealis, all of which he investigated; and a tall 18th Century barometer such as he used while charting the behavior of storms on land. In front of the model ship is a magnetized needle pushed through a cork; Franklin suggested that this device, floated in water, could act as a compass for shipwrecked mariners. He also studied magnets and their fields *(bottom, right)*; thoroughly described a mastodon's tooth dug up near the Ohio River *(bottom, center)*; reasoned, correctly, that coal was ancient vegetable matter buried by "convulsions of nature"; and concluded from examining fossil sea shells *(left of tooth)* that even the summits of the highest Appalachian Mountains had once been under water.

Defending himself against charges of fraudulently obtaining personal letters of Massachusetts' anticolonial royal governor, Franklin (at

AN HONEST AMERICAN, Franklin is shown being discovered by Diogenes, in a French print of 1780 *(below)*. His popularity in Paris was great and portraits of him were seen everywhere.

A RUSTIC SAGE in the eyes of the French, Franklin is pictured in his famous fur cap on this cover of a snuffbox, which joins him with their own revered philosophers Voltaire *(left)* and Rousseau.

left) stoically endures a harsh assault on his motives made before the Privy Council in 1774. Lord Shelburne called the attack "scurrilous."

Ambassador extraordinary

REPUBLICAN SIMPLICITY of Franklin's formal dress, which won French hearts, is portrayed in a rare watercolor *(below)*. Especially significant then was the lack of a ceremonial wig.

DURING most of 17 years, beginning in 1757, Franklin lived in London, serving variously as agent for Pennsylvania, Massachusetts, New Jersey and Georgia. He took up this role with affection for ancestral England and with a wide circle of English friends. But he grew disgusted with the general opinion that Americans were only second-class citizens. "Every man in England," he wrote, "seems to jostle himself into the throne with the king, and talks of *our subjects in the Colonies.*" During the stamp tax uproar he was asked: "Do not you think the people of America would submit to pay the stamp duty if it was moderated?" His answer was ominous: "No, never, unless compelled by force of arms."

When war came, Franklin was the logical choice to go to France and urge Louis XVI to be America's ally. His success in this mission was complete. And through his connections with printers and others, he set up a propaganda network which worked out so well that he could truthfully write, in 1777: "'Tis a Common Observation that our Cause is *the Cause of all Mankind,* and that we are fighting for their Liberty in defending our own."

FRANKLIN'S PHILADELPHIA lives on in Elfreth's Alley near the old waterfront. In one of these 18th Century houses dwelt William Maugridge, who helped Franklin start the Junto, a famous club devoted to singing, wine-drinking and self-improvement. The four-sided street lamps stem from a design by Franklin. To this kind of setting the ailing philosopher came home in 1785,

after being abroad for most of 30 years. He became president of the Executive Council of the Commonwealth of Pennsylvania, took a small part in writing the U.S. Constitution, and enjoyed some relaxed hours with his books and grandchildren. His funeral, in 1790, was attended by 20,000 people, the greatest procession ever assembled in Philadelphia up to that time.

7. THE REBELLION KINDLED

THE British Empire's behavior toward its colonies was extraordinary and paradoxical. To the settlers along the North Atlantic seaboard it generously granted home rule, and then tried to keep them from ruling at home. It counted on their loyalty to the empire, yet did not trust them to remain loyal. It regarded the colonists as English citizens, but denied them many of the basic rights of Englishmen. It insisted that the colonists assume their share of the burdens of empire, but would not let them have a serious voice in imperial decision-making. And by efficiently liberating them from threats of foreign attack, the British Empire made it far less necessary for itself to continue as a protector of the colonial peoples.

Even had the empire consisted only of the narrow American coastal strip between the Appalachians and the sea, its administration would have been complex and delicate. But by 1763, British territory sprawled from Hudson Bay to Borneo, from the Bay of Bengal to Honduras. This vast empire, comprising not 13 but 31 possessions, had been acquired in bits and pieces over 150 years. Its government was an administrative hodgepodge built up as new units were needed to cope with new problems as they came up. Some colonies —like the Hudson's Bay, the United East India, and the Royal African Companies—were run by private groups. Others—like Maryland, Pennsylvania and Delaware—were owned and governed by private proprietors. Only two of the 31—Connecticut and Rhode Island—still had self-governing status. One

ROBED AND RESPLENDENT, George III wears his coronation garb. American dislike of him dated from an early act authorizing indiscriminate searches of private homes.

colony after another had been brought under direct control of the crown, and the king's power was still growing. Along with Britain's West Indian islands, eight of the original 13 colonies were ruled by royal governors who controlled patronage and chose the upper houses of the legislatures.

Responsibility over colonial affairs never centered for long in any one governmental office. In 1696 the crown had established a Board of Trade and Plantations with broad supervisory power over commerce and colonies, though how much power the board actually exercised depended on the propensities and personal quirks of whoever happened to be in charge. After Lord Halifax became president in 1748, the board showed great vigor. After he left in 1761, it declined and in 1768 many of its functions were taken over by a Secretary of State for the Colonies. Colonial governors were appointed and directed by the office of Secretary of State for the Southern Department, whose main task was to conduct diplomatic relations with France and southern Europe. Under the Navigation Acts the Treasury Board had the function of collecting revenue. Their customs commissioners cooperated with the admiralty, whose naval officers had to check and clear colonial vessels. From 1697 vice admiralty judges named by the colonial governors and operating without juries heard maritime cases as well as suits concerning the trade acts, which involved not only commerce but such matters as the provision of ship timber for the crown. Until 1722 violations of the laws concerning ship timber were reported to the Surveyor General of the King's Woods in North America. But ordinary law courts in the colonies claimed an overlapping jurisdiction. Above all governmental bodies was the king's Privy Council, which, however, shared its authority with Parliament. And it was a resurgence of parliamentary power in the critical decade before 1775 which really precipitated the Revolution.

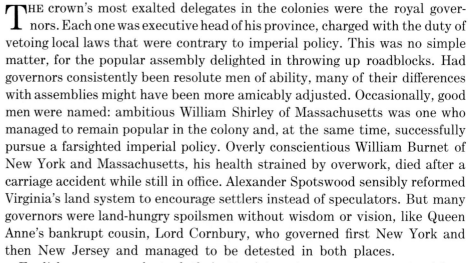

THE crown's most exalted delegates in the colonies were the royal governors. Each one was executive head of his province, charged with the duty of vetoing local laws that were contrary to imperial policy. This was no simple matter, for the popular assembly delighted in throwing up roadblocks. Had governors consistently been resolute men of ability, many of their differences with assemblies might have been more amicably adjusted. Occasionally, good men were named: ambitious William Shirley of Massachusetts was one who managed to remain popular in the colony and, at the same time, successfully pursue a farsighted imperial policy. Overly conscientious William Burnet of New York and Massachusetts, his health strained by overwork, died after a carriage accident while still in office. Alexander Spotswood sensibly reformed Virginia's land system to encourage settlers instead of speculators. But many governors were land-hungry spoilsmen without wisdom or vision, like Queen Anne's bankrupt cousin, Lord Cornbury, who governed first New York and then New Jersey and managed to be detested in both places.

English governors, who took their appointments as an easy way to riches, had no idea that in America they would be embroiled in a hot struggle for power similar to the long battle in Britain between the crown and Parliament. William Cosby, who governed New York from 1732 to 1736, confessed: "I have more trouble to manage these people than I could have imagined."

Public moneys in the colonies had to be raised through taxes voted by the assemblies. By loudly demanding all the rights of the House of Commons in England, the assemblies managed to wrest control over expenditures from the

The "London Magazine" bitterly pictured George III as a royal wastrel who frittered away George II's fat privy purse on "scoundrels who can thrum a vile piano, brush a picture, coop up a watch in a nut shell, or gild a calfskin." To refill his empty wallet, George counted on American taxes.

governors. Thus, in 1704, the New York assembly forced Lord Cornbury to turn tax money over to its own treasurer. Once the assembly controlled the purse strings, it was able to pay out or withhold salaries, including the governor's. Also, by voting salaries for only one year ahead at a time, the assembly virtually forced governors to select officials acceptable to it.

This kind of financial blackmail reached such a point that the New Jersey assembly made Governor Lewis Morris a bald offer of cash to sign a currency bill to pay salaries. Governor Morris, fortuitously blessed with a large private fortune, spurned the offer. But the assemblies seldom encountered so stanch —or so solvent—an adversary. Their tax and salary weapons quickly brought most governors to heel.

Assembly control over salaries led to a good deal of indirect influence over the courts, too. To combat this, the Board of Trade by the 1750s was instructing governors to commission judges "during the pleasure of the Crown" rather than "for good behavior," a phrase which meant they could be removed at any time on any pretext. From the colonists' point of view, this clearly undermined judicial independence, for it made judges more beholden to the king than to the colonists.

Possibly the assemblies might have been forced to toe the line, just as the judges were, had not colonial revenue and military support been desperately needed by England for the four wars against France between 1689 and 1763. This long struggle further accentuated the British Empire's constitutional difficulties with the colonies. The colonial empires of both France and England were involved. At stake in North America were not merely the teeming fisheries and the rich fur trade but future control of the vast, as yet largely unexplored, reaches of the continent. When hostilities began in 1689, Louis XIV of France was threatening to dominate all Europe. By 1763, England had decisively tipped the balance of power in its own favor.

In the Western Hemisphere fighting, France had certain notable advantages at the outset. Its empire was under strong central control, an immeasurable aid to quick decision-making. In the wilderness, where the war was largely to be fought, France possessed a network of Indian alliances stretching from Maine to Wisconsin. In the *coureurs de bois*, it had a ready-made cadre of scouts familiar with forests and trails, and experienced in dealing with the Indians. England, however, had an overwhelming superiority in the numbers of colonists and troops in America. The English navy dominated the seas. With more money than France to finance a war, and with more and cheaper trade goods to woo the Indians, England was able to expand its already existing alliance with the powerful Iroquois league.

THE four widely separated periods of Franco-English fighting followed a similar pattern. Each had three phases. First France would turn Indians loose against the exposed colonial frontiers. Then England would strike at French fortress cities in Canada with sea-borne forces. In the final phase each side would penetrate deep into the colonial holdings of the other. The colonists themselves and the individual colonies rarely acted in concert, responding only when their own particular safety or interest was threatened.

The first two of these conflicts—known in America as King William's War and Queen Anne's War—ended with Britain in possession of Newfoundland, Acadia and Hudson Bay. During the uneasy peace that followed, the French

As a colonial militia officer, George Washington pays a visit to Delaware Indian Queen Aliquippa while scouting French positions 22 years before Lexington. Washington reported that he "made her a present of a matchcoat and a bottle of rum, which latter was thought much the best present of the two."

relentlessly pressed their own settlement of the West. With Spanish help they stirred the Indians of the South and West to take the warpath against English settlers and traders. In the third intercolonial war, a joint expedition of New England soldiers commanded by William Pepperell and a British fleet under Sir Peter Warren seized Louisbourg on Cape Breton Island, the French bastion at the gateway to the St. Lawrence. This hard-won victory, in which dogged courage and plain good luck played equal parts, was thrown away afterward because France recovered Louisbourg with the stroke of a pen in the peace treaty of Aix-la-Chapelle in 1748.

THE treaty failed to settle matters finally between the major contestants. Both sides soon began preparing for a showdown. France rushed completion of a chain of forts, including one on Lake Ontario, another on Lake Erie and a third on the upper St. Lawrence. In the South and West, where they had founded New Orleans and St. Louis, they smoked the pipe of peace with the local Choctaws and along the Georgia and Carolina borders they sowed discord among the Chickasaws, Creeks and Cherokees. Meanwhile the English built Fort Oswego on Lake Ontario and encouraged the Iroquois through an Indian trader and land operator named William Johnson, who became the principal personage of the Mohawk Valley. Honorary sachem of the Mohawks, Johnson lived with them and married in the tribe. At the Albany Congress called in 1754 to discuss a unified defense by the colonies, the first order of business was a new treaty with the Indians. With 30 wagonloads of presents the English successfully mollified the touchy Iroquois chiefs and strengthened their alliance with military pledges as well. The congress also adopted a plan of colonial union proposed by Benjamin Franklin, but Britain was not prepared to go that far, and neither were the colonies—yet.

The French and Indian War, as the last bout of fighting is known in American history, was brought about by a race between France and England for control of the Ohio Valley. In 1753 Governor Dinwiddie of Virginia sent a 21-year-old militia officer named George Washington to Fort Venango, which the French had brashly built in western Pennsylvania, on the site of a former English trading post. Washington had a personal stake in the area because in 1749 he had surveyed it for a Virginia company developing a crown grant in the Ohio Valley. When Washington brought word that the French had politely turned down an ultimatum to vacate Venango, he was sent back by Dinwiddie to construct a fort at the site of present-day Pittsburgh. When he arrived he found that the French were already there, building Fort Duquesne. After defeating a French scouting party, he built a crude stockade nearby which he called Fort Necessity. The French thereupon overwhelmed Fort Necessity, and Washington was captured. Soon afterward he was released with the honors of war and returned home to Virginia.

Proudly promising to sweep the French out of the Ohio Valley, a British regular officer, General Edward Braddock, led two fine regiments through the woods of Pennsylvania in 1755. Washington, now a Virginia colonel, accompanied him at the head of nine companies of militiamen. Braddock doomed his soldiers from the start by insisting that, in the wilderness, they try to fight in a closed-rank style suitable only to open European fields and he used Indian scouts only sparingly. Ambushed by the French and Indians near Fort Duquesne, his forces were almost entirely destroyed. Washington managed to

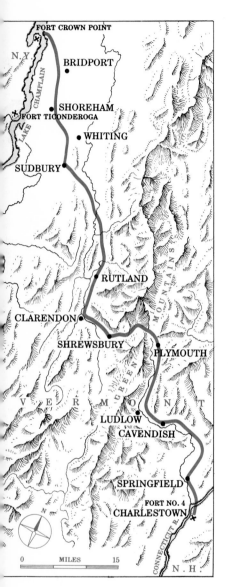

A HIGHWAY THAT LED
TO THE UNEXPECTED

In 1759 General Jeffrey Amherst captured the French fort at Crown Point (upper left) and at once set hundreds of troops to work cutting a road along an old Indian trail so he could bring up supplies from Fort No. 4, where Charlestown, New Hampshire (lower right), now stands. The French and Indian Wars ended before the road could be put to use, but sturdy pioneers took advantage of it to found settlements in what had been a wilderness. Then, in an ironic twist, during the Revolution Americans used the road to campaign against the British around Ticonderoga.

escape alive from the bloody ambuscade with 30 men of the three companies of Virginians who went into battle, plus four bullet holes in his coat, and a name for coolness which made him the talk of the empire. As a reward he was assigned the nearly impossible task of guarding a 400-mile frontier, from Maryland to North Carolina, with 1,500 untrained militia.

Thus America's rather informal shooting war began three years before the Seven Years' War in Europe, in which Austria joined with Russia and France against Prussia. George II, who besides being king of England was ruler of the German state of Hanover, allied himself with his former enemy Prussia to protect his German holdings. Both sides courted Spain, whose entry on France's side in 1762 came too late to be of much assistance. What began as a local quarrel over the Ohio Valley eventually spread to the West Indies, Europe, Africa and even to India.

In the fighting in North America, the French first captured Fort Oswego on Lake Ontario's south shore and Fort William Henry at the lower end of Lake George, sealing off the classic invasion routes to Canada, and seizing the military initiative. Fortunately for the colonies, at this difficult moment George II chose William Pitt, a man of extraordinary executive talents, as his chief minister. A manic depressive whose mood alternated between frenzied exaltation and darkest despondency, Pitt both formulated a grand strategy for the war and pursued it with relentless vigor. To tie down a major part of the French army in Europe, he provided strong British support for Prussia's Frederick the Great. He shook up the army in America, naming the youthful General James Wolfe as its commander. Louisbourg fell to British forces under Lord Jeffrey Amherst on July 26, 1758. A year later, General Wolfe's men scaled the sheer cliffs before Quebec and defeated the Marquis de Montcalm on the Plains of Abraham. Both generals died in the fighting. Montreal fell the following year, and in America it was all over.

The Treaty of Paris in 1763 eliminated France as a power in the New World. England acquired Canada and all French territory east of the Mississippi except New Orleans. In exchange for East and West Florida, England returned Cuba to Spain; and France, in a mood of unbounded generosity, gave its Spanish ally New Orleans and a vast uncharted empire (known as Louisiana) west of the Mississippi to compensate for whatever losses the Spanish had incurred in their brief moments of actual fighting. Of all its great North American empire, France retained only the two tiny fishing islands of St. Pierre and Miquelon near Newfoundland.

Long before boastful badmen took to notching their guns for every man they killed, the Indians were notching trees. Here Hendrick, a Mohawk sachem who sided with the British against the French, stands before a tree notched 39 times for enemies killed or captured. Hendrick, who once visited England, was killed in the first British effort to take Crown Point.

BRITAIN'S vastly enlarged empire would have challenged the imagination and audacity of gifted statesmen. The British politicians who now took office could not so be described, nor could their new king, whose weaknesses were to affect so crucially the future of the colonies. After ascending the throne in 1760, George III proved notably different from the earlier Hanoverians. He wanted to rule as well as reign, but had neither the temperament nor capacity for the role. His kingly manner concealed inner tension and a smoldering temper. Moralistic, snobbish, censorious, he combined a mulish inflexibility with an almost pathological conscientiousness in performing his duties. Moreover, a liver ailment caused him to suffer periods of insanity.

An effective opposition party might have provided a salutary check on the king's ministers. But the king was determined that his right to appoint and

dismiss ministers be unimpeded by the Commons. Because the Tories had long been discredited as traitors for their party's support of the exiled Stuarts, George III officially called himself a Whig. However, the splintered remnants of the great Whig oligarchy which had governed England for so long were not a party in the modern sense of the word, but a collection of small personal alliances. The "Old Whigs," centered around Lord Rockingham and Edmund Burke and at times allied with William Pitt, were the most sympathetic to the American colonies. Ignoring them, the king formed his own bloc, popularly known as the "King's Friends."

Such opposition as the king did meet with came from other Whigs. It did not succeed in blocking the king's ambitions, but the clash between these Whigs and the neoconservative elements which the king gathered around him created, after the parliamentary crisis touched off by the American Revolution, the basis for the two-party system that eventually emerged in England.

Many of the parliamentary evils that became noticeable under George III dated back for decades. The House of Commons needed drastic reorganization. Great population centers like London and the rising industrial cities of the Midlands either were grossly underrepresented in Parliament or had no voice at all. It was natural that men, such as Lord Shelburne, who sympathized most with the colonists' grievances were also the most urgent in pressing for reforms of suffrage and representation in England. To Shelburne, a liberal statesman who held Cabinet offices under Grenville and Pitt, taxation without representation was as angry a grievance at home as overseas.

George Grenville (above), a dour financier, was the prime minister who devised the stamps (below) to tax the colonies. In addition, Grenville vexed the king. He insulted George's mother by trying to exclude her as a prospective regent and he demanded economies even at Buckingham Palace. He did not last in office long enough to see the storm break over his stamps.

THE transatlantic conflict of wills which culminated in the Revolution is usually confined by historians to the decade just before 1775. But colonial discontent had long been smoldering. During the French and Indian War, British customs officials had tried to cut off the vast illegal trade the colonists carried on with the enemy in Canada and the West Indies. Traditional warrants authorized search only in the places specified on the warrant and upon explicit information. But using the war emergency as justification, general warrants—or writs of assistance—were issued to let customs officers search anywhere for smuggled goods without requiring them to present reasons for suspecting illicit items. There was little opposition to them at the time. But when George III became king, all the old writs, issued in his grandfather's name, expired and new ones had to be applied for. In Boston this touched off the celebrated Writs of Assistance Case.

Nobody now bothers to recall the names of any of the 63 merchants who opposed issuance of the writs. But the arguments made in court against the writs by an impassioned New England lawyer named James Otis have a cherished place in American history. John Adams, who attended the trial and reported it in his diary, wrote that Otis "was a flame of fire." The lawyer denounced the writs as "instruments of slavery," and insisted that, even had Parliament authorized the writs, "an act against the Constitution is void" and could be set aside by the courts because of man's natural right to liberty. "Then and there," Adams later concluded, "the child Independence was born."

The trial judges delayed taking action for almost a year. Finally, pressure from Chief Justice Thomas Hutchinson forced them to grant the writs, despite continued protest by the colonists. However, the writs were successfully resisted in other colonies when specifically authorized by Parliament in 1767. In

Pennsylvania Chief Justice William Allen refused to allow them to be used because they were "not Warranted by Law." The battle over the writs elevated the controversy between colonies and mother country from the level of bickering over taxes to the loftier plane of a searching inquiry into personal liberty. In its 1776 Bill of Rights, Virginia was to condemn the writs as "grievous and oppressive." Five other revolutionary states were to resist them successfully and a prohibition against them was incorporated into the Fourth Amendment to the Federal Constitution.

ANOTHER suit which exacerbated feelings between mother country and colonies was "The Parson's Cause" of 1763, a case involving the Reverend James Maury. This had its origins back in 1755. At that time the need to raise funds to maintain frontier defenses had impelled the Virginia colony's burgesses to adopt a discriminatory bill, known as the Two Penny Act, which in effect made Church of England clergy in Virginia pay more than their fair share of the defense tax. For almost a century, the ministers had been paid in pounds of tobacco. The Two Penny Act recalculated these salaries at the rate of two pence per pound. The market price of tobacco was actually double or treble the legislature's rate, and the clergymen fought back, taking their case to the Privy Council in London, which disallowed the Virginia act in 1759.

Not content with this victory, Maury sued the colony in 1763 for back pay. Though morally justified, his suit became a much-publicized test case that merely succeeded in antagonizing Virginia's aristocratic laity. Opposing the minister's claim was a hot-blooded spellbinder named Patrick Henry, who only three years before, after trying his hand at farming and storekeeping, had put up his lawyer's shingle outside his father-in-law's tavern. Henry charged that the king in disallowing the Two Penny Act had, "from being the Father of his people, degenerated into a Tyrant," forfeiting thereby "all right to his subjects' Obedience." This was strong language for 1763, but the court did not rebuke the young attorney, and the jury, ignoring evidence that the plaintiff suffered damages of £288, returned a nominal verdict which in effect defied the Privy Council: Maury recovered just one penny in damages.

Frontier conditions played a part in building colonial resentments against London. The expulsion of France from North America had created a power vacuum in the huge territory stretching south from the Hudson's Bay Company's domain to the Gulf of Mexico and west from the Alleghenies to the Mississippi. The war had hardly ended when the frontier was again ablaze. The western Indians, victimized by fraudulent land deals and crowded out of their lands by the steady tide of settlement, went on the warpath in 1763 under the leadership of the Ottawa chief Pontiac. They captured every army post on the frontier except Niagara, Detroit and Fort Pitt. The uprising was put down largely with colonial troops recruited and paid for by the colonists themselves.

Pontiac's rebellion imparted a terrible sense of urgency to the western problem. Decisive action was needed in London. Instead, the British government offered a makeshift and impractical solution—to reserve all the territory of the West for the Indians. The idea appealed to businessmen in London, who believed that if the colonists could be confined to the coastal areas, they might continue to be more economically dependent on the mother country. The youthful Shelburne, head of the Board of Trade, recommended that the Appalachians, save for a projected colonial settlement in the upper Ohio, should

"The Pennsylvania Journal," protesting the Stamp Act, announced that it was "expiring" and printed a skull and crossbones (above). A special Stamp Act congress sent the king a petition to withdraw the stamps. It was signed (below) by Otis of Massachusetts, Borden of New Jersey, Livingston of New York, and Gadsden and Rutledge of South Carolina, among others.

stand as a temporary boundary between the colonies and an Indian reservation. This stopgap plan was duly adopted. Later British ministries came to consider the line of demarcation a permanent barrier to westward expansion, but in America it was a line and nothing more. "Long hunters," led by Daniel Boone, and entrepreneurs like John Sevier and James Robertson, who in 1772 organized a *de facto* state in what would later be Tennessee, paid no attention to it. Soon settlers were pouring west over the Wilderness Trail. But the ministry's arbitrary boundary put a crimp in some of the grandiose plans of land speculators from Virginia and Pennsylvania, and exasperated influential colonists whom the British could ill afford to antagonize.

Britain found that the protracted struggle with the French had doubled the national debt. To reduce the debt, to meet the ordinary costs of government and the additional burdens imposed by vast new acquisitions, the king had to find more money. Since the British taxpayer had demonstrated by rioting over a new cider tax that he had reached the limits of his willingness or ability to pay, the king decided that the colonists should assume the additional tax load. The old system of levying requisitions on the colonies had largely broken down. Colonial legislatures set so high a price for cooperating that royal governors had found it meant surrendering their freedom of action. "America is not used to great taxes," John Adams observed. "The people . . . are not yet disciplined to such enormous taxation as in England."

To get the desired money a new ministry headed by George Grenville proposed a tariff to be imposed by Parliament. This was a modification of the old Molasses Act of 1733. The heavy duties the old act imposed on sugar, rum and molasses from the Spanish and French islands in the West Indies were designed to discourage trade rather than to raise revenue. It had signally failed to change a well-rooted trade pattern; American merchants continued to trade in the most advantageous market even if it meant smuggling or conniving with corrupt customs officials. Fortunately for the colonists, the British customs service in America was both venal and indulgent. In Boston officials usually settled for about one tenth of the legal duty on foreign molasses; in New York, for a fourth. Even at that, scarcely a trickle of the duty collected reached the royal treasury. Grenville's Sugar Act of 1764, while it modified the Molasses Act, stated its real aim as being to raise revenue in the colonies "toward defraying the necessary expenses of defending, protecting, and securing the said colonies." A companion measure provided for tighter enforcement of the revenue laws. Still another, prohibiting the issue of legal tender currency in all the American colonies, alienated Southerners.

G RENVILLE coupled his proposal for a tax on exports and imports with a scheme to levy a tax *within* the colonies through stamp duties—to be placed on newspapers, almanacs, pamphlets and broadsides, legal documents, ship's papers, licenses—even on dice and playing cards. Such taxes had often been used in England. In a few cases similar duties had been imposed by colonial legislatures. But as an internal levy on the colonists imposed by a distant parliament in which the colonists had no representation, the Stamp Act of 1765 was even less supportable constitutionally than the Sugar Act.

The Sugar Act aroused merchants. The Stamp Act, because it touched everyone's pocketbook, aroused everyone. All sorts of groups started their own special boycotts. Merchants banned the importation of British goods. Lawyers

WILLIAM JACKSON,

an *IMPORTER*; at the

BRAZEN HEAD,

North Side of the TOWN-HOUSE,

and *Oppofite the Town-Pump, in*

Corn-hill, BOSTON.

It is defired that the SONS and DAUGHTERS of *LIBERTY,* would not buy any one thing of him, for in fo doing they will bring Difgrace upon *themfelves,* and their *Pofterity,* for *ever* and *ever,* AMEN.

With this placard, patriot leaders asked Bostonians to boycott a merchant selling British goods. As a proof of patriotism, Americans refused to wear British garments. Classes at Harvard and Princeton received degrees in homespun.

turned out a succession of devastating pamphlet attacks on the Grenville measures. One way and another, a terrible clamor arose. James Otis was the first to raise the question of "taxation without representation." The English quickly branded this an absurd idea. A British pamphleteer, Soame Jenyns, asked if the Americans were not virtually represented by members of Parliament acting for the whole empire. Replying angrily, Maryland lawyer Daniel Dulany called the notion of "virtual" representation "a mere cob-web, spread to catch the unwary and intangle the weak." Dulany carefully distinguished the Stamp Act from other revenue measures on the ground that it was an internal tax levied for "the single purpose of revenue." In the Virginia House of Burgesses, Patrick Henry furiously warned George III to remember the fates of Caesar and Charles I. The assembly rejected Henry's more extreme assertions but endorsed his general principle: no taxation without representation. This stand was also upheld by delegates from nine colonies meeting in New York in 1765.

FED a steady diet of incendiary exhortation by the hostile press, skillfully directed by respectable merchants and lawyers through local groups known as Sons of Liberty (a term coined by Colonel Isaac Barré in Parliament), the American people took to violence. In Boston Sam Adams—who combined a statesman's vision with a politician's talent for rabble-rousing—shrewdly kept the pot boiling. Mobs burned the records of the vice admiralty court, looted the home of the Comptroller of Customs, pillaged and sacked the elegant residence of Chief Justice Thomas Hutchinson. "Our Presses have groaned," John Adams summed it up, "our Pulpits have thundered, our Legislatures have resolved, our Towns have voted, the Crown Officers have every where trembled." General Thomas Gage, commander of the British forces which were a constant irritation to the colonists, wrote home that the colonies had swallowed an overdose of "the Spirit of Democracy." Every one of the royally appointed stamp agents quit before November 1, the effective date of the Stamp Act, save Georgia's stamp distributor. He arrived furtively in the colony, briefly looked around and soon left for parts unknown.

The *Boston Gazette* offered George Grenville this couplet:

> To make us all Slaves, now you've lost Sir! the Hope,
> You've but to go hang yourself.—We'll find the Rope.

Then George III turned on poor Grenville—for another reason. Grenville had proposed a bill which gave the king power to appoint a regent if he himself should become incapacitated. The bill specifically excluded the king's mother as prospective regent because she was widely reputed to be the mistress of Lord Bute. Grenville and others feared that if the king's mother were to become regent, Bute, the most hated man in British politics, would, in effect, be king. Wielding his bloc of votes in Parliament, the king overturned his prime minister and had his mother's name written into the bill. But he never forgave

The separated serpent on the masthead of the "Massachusetts Spy" (below), bidding the colonies unite, drew the gibes of Tory wits. They sang: "Ye sons of Sedition, how comes it to pass / That America's typed by a snake—in the grass?"

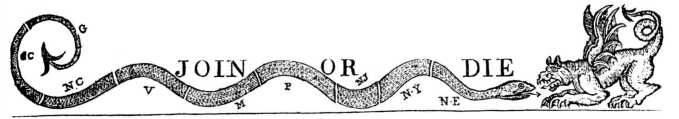

Grenville. The next ministry—headed by Lord Rockingham—had to tidy up the mess left by its predecessors. Complicating matters was the rage of British merchants, who were owed huge sums by American businessmen and whose prospects for collection were greatly diminished when trade with America dropped almost 14 per cent as a result of colonial boycotts.

The struggle in Parliament was as fierce as it was in Boston. When Grenville denounced the colonists as "ungrateful," Pitt exclaimed, "I rejoice that America has resisted." Yet, Pitt demanded that "the authority of this Kingdom over the colonies . . . be Sovereign and Supreme" and "made to extend to every point of Legislation whatsoever; that we may bind their Trade, confine their Manufactures, and exercise every Power whatsoever, except that of taking the Money out of their Pockets without their Consents." This proved Pitt understood America's temper little better than Grenville. Rockingham had the Stamp Act repealed, but the ministry tacked on to the repeal a Declaratory Act asserting Parliament's unbounded right to legislate for the colonies. Like Pitt, even the moderates in Parliament failed to realize the colonies were objecting not so much to the weight of taxes as to Parliament's power to tax.

"The Great Commoner," William Pitt, now become Earl of Chatham, was sure he understood America. "You must repeal her fears . . ." he told Parliament. "You may then hope for her love and gratitude." He died (1778) without ever realizing that the issue was not taxes. The colonies wanted independence.

John Dickinson had brilliantly set forth the case for America in his "Letters from a Farmer in Pennsylvania to the Inhabitants of the British colonies," but he believed in conciliation. This moved John Adams to call him a "piddling genius." Later Dickinson was to fight well in Washington's army.

W HEN the Rockingham ministry fell apart, it was Pitt's turn to govern. But the Great Commoner—now in the House of Lords as the Earl of Chatham, his nerves shattered, his health impaired—deputized the Duke of Grafton to organize a makeshift coalition in which the Chancellor of the Exchequer would play a larger role in colonial affairs. When witty and reckless Charles Townshend (Champagne Charlie) was given that post, Horace Walpole, a literary Parliamentarian, observed: "He [would have] had almost every great talent . . . if he had had but common truth, common sincerity, common honesty, common modesty, common steadiness, common courage and common sense." Americans of the stature of Dulany, Hutchinson and Franklin had protested Parliament's right to impose internal taxes. Well and good, reasoned Townshend: he would let the colonists have a dose of external taxes. The Townshend Acts of 1767 thereupon imposed duties on a long list of imports, including glass, paper, tea, lead and paints. Townshend's aim was to use the receipts for "defraying the charge of the administration of justice, and . . . government, in such provinces where it shall be found necessary." Anything left over could help pay the costs of maintaining troops in America.

The new revenue measure unleashed another pamphlet war and another series of boycotts. In his formidable *Letters from a Farmer in Pennsylvania*, which won an enormous readership, the moderate Whig attorney John Dickinson denied Parliament's right to impose any tax to raise revenue in America. Early in 1768, Sam Adams and James Otis got the Massachusetts House of Representatives to denounce the Townshend Acts as a violation of the principle of no taxation without representation. Governor Francis Bernard dissolved the assembly but other colonies endorsed the stand of Massachusetts. When the Virginia legislature urged support for the Bay Colony, Governor Botetourt dismissed the burgesses. They met next day informally at the Raleigh Tavern in Williamsburg and promptly adopted a nonimportation agreement. In a few months exports from England to America slumped 38 per cent.

Taxation remained the immediate issue. But militarism became a pervading grievance. Instead of reducing its forces in America after the war, England had stationed some 10,000 regular troops there. Quartering acts passed in

1765 and 1774 required private homes to provide billeting facilities for British soldiers in the colonies. Why, if the troops were needed to secure the new frontiers, the colonists asked, were most regiments based in and around the larger cities? New York was the first headquarters of what colonists came to consider an army of occupation. That city was first to voice opposition. The New York Assembly refused full compliance with the quartering acts, whereupon Governor Sir Henry Moore dismissed it. In 1766 and again early in 1770, redcoats clashed on the streets with New York "Liberty Boys."

In Boston, John Adams observed, "certain busy characters [tried] between the inhabitants of the lower class and the soldiers . . . to enkindle an immortal hatred." Economic rivalry intensified this mutual animosity. Boston workmen resented the soldiers' taking off-duty jobs at low wages to eke out their scanty military pay. On March 2, 1770, a fight broke out between Boston journeymen and some British privates seeking work. On March 5, a mob taunted a squad of redcoats, and the exasperated soldiery fired. Exploited for all it was worth by skillful propagandists, this "Boston Massacre" infuriated the colonists. Even so, the accused soldiers got a fair trial. Two of the colony's ablest attorneys, the patriot leaders John Adams and Josiah Quincy Jr., assumed the unpopular defense from a stern sense of duty and secured the acquittal of Captain Thomas Preston, the commanding officer, and six men. Two others were found guilty of manslaughter. The tragic event deepened colonial distrust of standing armies, which was one of the grievances to be enumerated in the Declaration of Independence. (As John Adams bluntly put it to patriot General Horatio Gates in 1776: "We dont choose to trust you Generals with too much Power for too long a time.")

"From that moment," Daniel Webster later asserted of the Boston Massacre, "we may date the severance of the British Empire." But though the incident further poisoned the air, it did not actually set off the war. For a few years, tension even relaxed. Parliament again backtracked and repealed every Townshend tax save the one on tea. The colonists dropped their boycott. Some rich merchants, disturbed by the mob spirit which had been unleashed, moved away from the extremist positions held by irreconcilable radicals like Sam Adams in Boston, Isaac Sears and Alexander McDougall in New York, Christopher Gadsden in Charleston. Some of the wealthiest businessmen, however, had been the victims of vengeful prosecution by customs officials. Many of these colonials considered the customs officers little better than blackmailers and extortionists. Merchants of this persuasion engaged in illicit operations with the non-British West Indies. And they bided their time.

IN June 1772, while pursuing a merchant ship, the customs schooner *Gaspee* ran aground at Namquit Point near Providence. At nightfall John Brown, a rich Rhode Island merchant, led an attack on the schooner by eight boatloads of muscle men from Providence. The *Gaspee's* captain was shot, its crew was removed and the ship set afire. An inquiry failed to turn up any tangible evidence. No one recognized anybody.

The tension began to build again. Not long after the *Gaspee* inquiry, Governor Hutchinson of Massachusetts abruptly announced that he would thereafter be paid by the crown instead of by legislative appropriation. A few months later a similar declaration was made with regard to Massachusetts judges. Sam Adams, alarmed at this reassertion of the independence of the

Thomas Paine, an Englishman who never saw America until 1774, wrote the Revolution's most effective pamphlets urging American independence. His scorn for "summer soldiers and sunshine patriots," heartening the Continental troops before the stunning battle of Trenton, helped to win the day.

Thomas Hutchinson, royal governor of Massachusetts, came from one of New England's old families, but he sided with the king and died abroad. He was a fiscal expert, and John Adams later wished he could "wake the ghost of Hutchinson and give him absolute power over the currency of the U.S."

royal executive and the judiciary from colonial legislative control, pushed through a Boston town meeting a resolution to appoint a Committee of Correspondence to communicate Boston's position on public problems to other towns and "to the World." This was the first effective revolutionary machinery. By early 1774, every colony but Pennsylvania had similar committees.

It would seem that the British ministries could have gauged the rising danger. After the imposition of every tax, they had been forced to backtrack. "What enforcing and what repealing; what bullying and what submitting; what doing and undoing," thundered Edmund Burke in Commons. And Burke knew. His editorial work for the *Annual Register*, London's informative news bulletin, his services as a colonial agent for New York and, perhaps more important, his role as an Opposition spokesman in Parliament, all required close knowledge of what was going on in America. But ignoring its history of reversing itself, Parliament refused to abandon the right to tax.

Lord North was, in a colleague's words, a "great, heavy, booby looking" fellow with prominent, darting eyes. He boasted that he was a man of high principle who never voted for a popular measure in his life. He insisted on keeping the tax on tea to assert the principle that Great Britain had a right to tax America—and so, as a matter of principle, he brought on the war.

IN the spring of 1773 the East India Company, a quasi-governmental enterprise, was in serious financial difficulty. To stave off disaster, the government proposed giving the company a monopoly of the tea trade with America, free of the ordinary British duties but retaining the tax of three pence per pound paid in America. Since the company also could sell directly to agents in the colonies, colonists would pay less for tea but the East India Company would have a big competitive edge over colonial merchants who had bought tea at higher prices or had smuggled it in from Holland. Yet it was the threat of monopoly, not the tax, that aroused the colonists. The inventors of this "noble piece of chicanery," Benjamin Franklin charged, "have no idea that any people can act from any other principle but that of interest; and they believe [this small reduction] sufficient to overcome all the patriotism of an American."

In most colonial ports, unloaded tea was placed in warehouses to keep it out of commerce, or the tea ships were forbidden to land their cargoes. But in this, as in so much else, Boston was different. Governor Thomas Hutchinson, whose two sons and a nephew happened to be consignees of the East India Company, refused to let the *Dartmouth* and two other tea ships clear Boston harbor for England unless the duty on the unloaded tea was paid. On the evening of December 16, 1773, "Mohawk braves" had their famous "tea party" on the ships. The contents of 342 chests of tea tumbled into the harbor, and John Adams confessed that "Many Persons wish, that as many dead Carcasses were floating in the Harbour, as there are Chests of Tea."

A wrathful ministry now pushed through Parliament a series of laws which Americans called the Intolerable Acts. Over the eloquent and farsighted objections of Chatham and Burke, the port of Boston was shut down until the Company had been paid and the customs collected for the drowned tea leaves. A second act permitted anyone indicted in the colonies for a capital offense committed in putting down a riot or collecting revenue to be tried in England or another colony to insure an unprejudiced trial. A third measure in effect annulled the Massachusetts charter by bolstering the governor's power, weakening the colonial assembly and drastically curtailing town meetings. A more extensive quartering act, even more unpalatable than its predecessor, followed. Finally, the Quebec Act of 1774 provided for the civil government of Canada and extended its boundaries southward to the Ohio River, thereby nullifying all land claims of the original Thirteen Colonies to the Northwest.

The other American colonies now joined ranks with Massachusetts. Colonial intellectuals took up a far more extreme position on independence. Thomas Jefferson, a talented planter and attorney from upcountry Virginia; James Wilson, a Scottish immigrant with a law practice on the Pennsylvania frontier; Alexander Hamilton, a youthful prodigy who dropped his studies at King's College to give full time to forwarding the colonial cause; and stout John Adams—all were in substantial agreement. No one expressed this radical position more forcefully or persuasively than Jefferson, who as a burgess from Albemarle County had quickly won recognition in his native Virginia as a skillful literary draftsman. In his powerful "Summary View of the Rights of British America," Jefferson described the king as merely the "Chief Magistrate" of the empire and urged him to heed "liberal and expanded thought." Parliament, Jefferson insisted, not only had no right to tax the colonies, it had no authority over the colonies whatsoever.

Even moderates like George Washington felt that with these latest royal measures things had gone too far for petitions. "Shall we, after this, whine and cry for relief, when we have already tried it in vain?" he wrote in July 1774.

British coercion had brought about what a decade of laborious agitation had failed to create—a union among the Thirteen Colonies for resistance. In response to resolutions of Virginia and Massachusetts, a congress met at Philadelphia on September 5, 1774. The First Continental Congress was to become, in John Adams' phrase, "a nursery of American Statesmen." The 56 delegates ranged from passionate radicals like Patrick Henry to extreme conservatives like the vain and adroit Joseph Galloway of Pennsylvania who teetered on the brink of loyalism toward the crown.

The radicals scored first. Congress denounced the English laws as unconstitutional, advising the people to arm and set up their own militia, and recommended stiff economic sanctions against Britain. The conservatives countered with a plan of union proposed by Galloway, a watered-down version of Franklin's Albany Plan, which was narrowly defeated, by six votes to five. From here on, the radicals had it all their own way. A Continental Association was established to implement a total boycott of British goods. Congress denied that Parliament had any legislative authority over the colonies. It endorsed an "Address to the People of Great Britain," a moving and dignified appeal written by John Jay, a wealthy young lawyer of New York, and sent it to the mother country along with John Dickinson's moderate petition directed to the king himself. Perhaps most important of all, Congress agreed to meet again on May 10, 1775, if American wrongs had not by then been redressed.

Edmund Burke, a Whig spokesman, poured scorn on North's policies. "You will never see a shilling from America," he predicted. But America found him a perplexing friend, for Burke held as strongly as North that England's Parliament was the supreme power in America. But he wanted Parliament to bind the colonies to England by a mild use of its authority.

WHEN Chatham moved in the Lords for the withdrawal of the troops in America, he was thrust aside, Franklin commented bitterly, as though his motion were a "ballad offered by a drunken porter." In November 1774, George III wrote his prime minister, "The New England governments are in a state of rebellion. . . ." And outside occupied Boston, patriot minutemen were drilling and military stores were being collected. At the moment, the citizen soldiers were rallying to fight the home government for their rights as Englishmen. But Americans, whose warranted confidence in their ability to govern themselves had brought them to this decisive point, were forging a new and distinctive American nationality that would prove its strength in the coming fight for independence.

IN SPITEFUL SATIRE England hits back at American women, whose boycotts hurt its economy. This 1775 London cartoon portrays North Carolinians signing patriotic pledges while wearing smuggled finery, flirting and abandoning a baby to a dog's care.

Fiery days of the Sons of Liberty

KING GEORGE III's Americans had ever been quick to defend their ancient English liberties; his English had let theirs erode. This important difference eluded both the king and his ministers when they levied taxes to force the colonies to pay a share of the expensive Seven Years' War (1756-1763) that had added India, Canada and all America east of the Mississippi (except New Orleans) to the British crown. Furious over what they considered a betrayal of their rights as Englishmen, defiant Americans fought against the taxes even though they risked hanging for their resistance.

Afterward, it was difficult to tell just when colonists ceased to be loyal English subjects outraged over taxes imposed from abroad and became outright rebels. Many, perhaps a third of them, remained forever loyal to England. But others, at first a few, then more and more, warmed only to ideas of freedom. They called themselves Sons of Liberty, formed secret societies to push and persuade neighbors onto the path for independence, and set up Committees of Correspondence to tell their troubles to each other and the world. From the king's coronation to Lexington and Concord, the arguments grew yearly more bitter. They flared late in jeering English attacks *(above)* on patriotic American women who refused to buy English goods, exploded early in the raging rhetoric of Patrick Henry *(right)* crying to the House of Burgesses that only Virginia (later he would say America) had the right to tax Virginians.

IN DARING ORATORY, Patrick Henry offers his "Resolves" in 1765. Branding as enemies any outsiders who tried to tax Virginians, Henry, it is said, shouted: "If this be treason make the most of it!" In this painting an artist has romanticized him, with arm outflung and a gauntlet of defiance cast upon the floor. The heated "Resolves" lit answering fires in every colony.

JAMES OTIS, opposing search warrants in 1761 *(right)*, declares that man has natural rights no king can infringe. John Adams said that this was when independence was born.

THE COUNCIL CHAMBER in the Old Town House *(opposite)* is much as it was when James Otis eloquently presented the case against the royal infringement of the colonies' rights.

The natural law and America's reluctant heroes

WITH some notable exceptions the leading Sons of Liberty were heroes only intermittently. In his Old Town House speech, the brilliant James Otis set forth the fundamental concepts of natural law that raised the dispute with Britain from a squabble over taxes to an assault by despotic government on the sacred rights of man. Later, he begged protection of the royal governor, smashed windows in Town House and went mad. The Virginians who adopted Patrick Henry's "Resolves" took some of the fire out of them the minute he was out of town, and at times nearly all the great men of the Carolinas, Pennsylvania and New York—even Massachusetts' John Adams and John Hancock—had their waverings.

Most notable of the exceptions was John Adams' cousin Sam, the grand incendiary and indefatigable propagandist of the Revolution. There was little prudence in Sam Adams' patriotism; at home in turbulent Boston, he had learned his politics in its cantankerous caucus clubs, forerunners of all the smoke-filled rooms in American history. When the scent of freedom came into the air, he was everywhere. He hammered courage into overcautious leaders and mobilized the bully boys who brawled in Boston's streets. Wherever rebellion boiled—in the Stamp Act riots, the Boston Massacre, the Boston Tea Party, and in organizing the powerful Committees of Correspondence—somewhere near the center stood Sam.

THE TIRELESS PROPAGANDIST Sam Adams is shown with Massachusetts' charter. Otis was his superior in the colonial assembly, but after 1765 Sam was Boston's real boss.

When words yielded to bonfires and bullets

A STAMP ACT RIOT takes place in the South. In every colony Sons of Liberty burned the stamps, beat up the tax officials, wrecked their offices and made them apologize to the public.

WITH the Stamp Act of 1765, the crisis exploded from courts and congresses into the streets. The stamps, which were to be bought and affixed to newspapers, legal documents and other public papers, constituted a mild tax. But the levy came as depression succeeded the brief boom that followed the Seven Years' War. It pinched influential groups—lawyers, publishers, tavernkeepers and merchants—and led them to wink at rowdy protest. In Boston, there emerged more aggressive Sons of Liberty, such as Paul Revere, the up-and-coming silversmith; Crispus Attucks, the giant Negro patriot; George Robert Twelvetrees Hewes, the tiny street brawler. Elsewhere other opponents of the tax came forward. For three astonishing months starting in August 1765, they used public humiliations to force every stamp agent in America to quit, chased English troops off the streets of Charleston, New York and Boston, and nullified royal power even in cities where the English maintained garrisons.

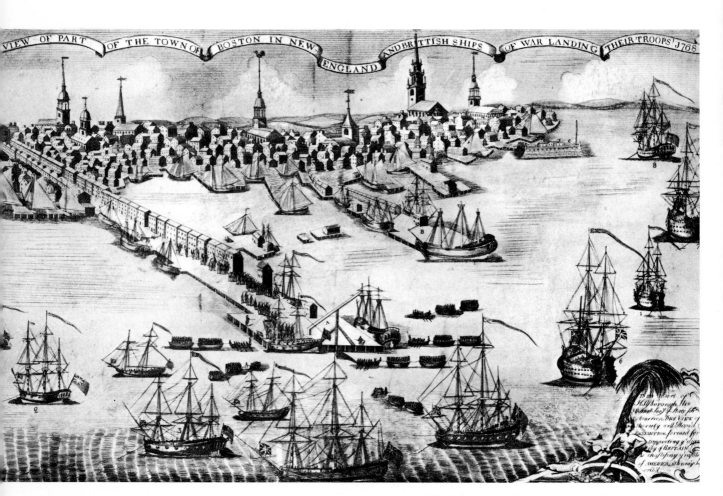

A ROYAL REPLY to the increasing turbulence comes when two British regiments debark on Boston's Long Wharf in 1768 under orders to "rescue the government from the hands of a trained mob." Paul Revere made the engravings above and opposite to stir wrath against British oppression. Long before his memorable ride, he was a skilled propagandist for the Sons of Liberty.

THE BOSTON MASSACRE is recorded in Revere's engraving of a clash between a street mob and English troops in 1770. It is a propaganda classic. In truth, there was of course no sign reading "Butcher's Hall" on the English customs house. It was the mob that started the fight, not the troops. British Captain Preston was not waving his sword, but trying to stop the brawl.

161

The English schooner "Gaspee," gone aground while chasing a smuggler near Providence in 1772, gives the patriots a golden opportunity.

Threatening portents of a fast-gathering storm

PERIPHERAL lightning flickered around the growing storm. By siding with the royal governor in his war against vigilante-like bands of small, western farmers, called Regulators, the patriot plantation owners of the North Carolina seacoast lost in 1771 allies they would need in 1775. But all along the seaboard British officials mobilized hosts of spies, searchers, warships, customs

Eight boatloads of them in Indian dress rowed out and burned her.

A BLUSTERY GOVERNOR, William Tryon *(above)* faces angry Regulators in New Bern, North Carolina. These rioters fought the unfair taxation and official greed that plagued their lives.

A CALM PATRIOT, Abraham Whipple *(below)* shows the control that enabled him to tell the British to catch him first when they promised to hang him for his part in the *Gaspee* affair.

commissioners and admiralty judges to fight smuggling, and thereby created new patriots. For Americans, as the English said, smuggled by instinct. They considered it virtuous, for besides bringing large profits, it defrauded wicked England. John Hancock, caught smuggling, tossed the agents into Boston harbor, landed his cargo of wine and swore he would never drink tax-polluted stuff.

"PAYING THE EXCISEMAN" portrays a patriot reprisal that was twice visited on Johnny Malcolm, a spy for British customs. In Maine Johnny was caught, tarred and feathered, but with his clothes on. Later, in Boston, he taunted the street crowds for a bad job. So they stripped him naked, refeathered him and made him toast in tea all 11 members of the royal family.

164

At the Boston Tea Party, one of the stirring incidents of the period, patriots garbed as Mohawks throw the hated leaves into the harbor.

Hateful taxes and the smell of tar and feathers

IN a conciliatory effort, Parliament in 1770 repealed all the irksome duties save that on tea. The New York merchants ended their boycott. But in 1773 this amiable mood was broken when the bumbling British officials decided to sell taxed tea cheaper than the smugglers could afford to sell the smuggled leaves. Everywhere, outraged patriots burned the taxed tea or threw it into the water, and the spirit of resistance blazed up again.

A HOISTED TAXMAN appears in an illustration for a poem. And a Tory, M'Fingal, who protested the deed, becomes the next victim of the crowd. He is bound to the bottom of the pole.

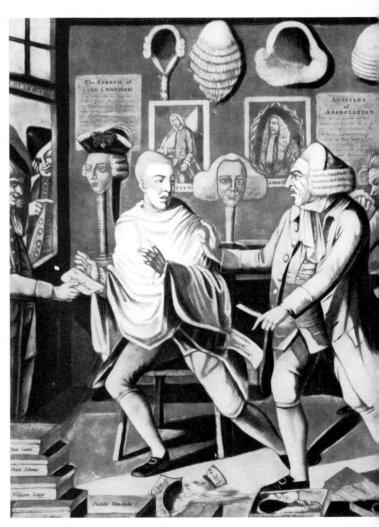

"THE PATRIOTICK BARBER" celebrates the uncompromising attitude of Jacob Vredenburg who, on discovering his client to be a British naval officer, sent him half-shaven to the street.

165

A foretaste of America's resolute desire for liberty

A grave general, Thomas Gage listens to a youthful delegation. The scene is part of an amiable legend which starts with the general's arrival in Boston in 1774 under orders to punish the town until it paid for the tea it had fed the fish. Before him stood these schoolboys to demand satisfaction because redcoats had smashed their snow forts. He is supposed to have murmured: "The very children here draw in a love of liberty with the air they breathe."

But no one had to tell Tom Gage much about America. A veteran of 17 years in the colonies, he was related, by his marriage to an American, to Philip Schuyler, a leading Son of Liberty. James Otis was his friend; so was George Washington. They all knew him for a decent, good-natured man who would let the children have their snow forts, but who believed in, and would enforce, every decree Britain might impose on America. Pursuing his duty, Gage would soon be facing some of his old friends, now foes, on the field of battle.

The Revolution, with its terrible trials and its torturing conflicts of loyalty, would test men's will to freedom in fratricidal war.

CHRONOLOGY *A timetable of American and world events: Before 1775*

WORLD EVENTS	EXPLORATION and SETTLEMENT	POLITICS	MILITARY	ECONOMICS and SCIENCE	RELIGION, ARTS and PEOPLE
c. 40,000-10,000 B.C. Cro-Magnon Man	**c. 35,000-20,000 B.C.** First migrants from Asia reach North America				**c. 8000 B.C.** Folsom man makes tools in Southwest
1000-431 B.C. Greek city states flourish					

Christian Era

WORLD EVENTS	EXPLORATION and SETTLEMENT	POLITICS	MILITARY	ECONOMICS and SCIENCE	RELIGION, ARTS and PEOPLE
1066-72 A.D. Normans conquer England	**1000 A.D.** Leif Ericsson discovers Vinland				**c. 900-1300 A.D.** Mound-Builder empire centered on Cahokia flourishes in Mississippi Valley
1450-1550 Renaissance	**1492** Columbus makes first voyage to New World				**1000** Pueblo Indians withdraw to canyon and cliff communities
1453-1585 Ottoman Empire	**1497** John Cabot explores North American coast			**c. 1500** Europeans start fishing off North American coast	**c. 1000-1450** Maya civilization flourishes in Yucatán
1517 Luther's 95 theses set off Reformation	**1513** Juan Ponce de Leon discovers Florida				**1325-1519** Aztec civilization reaches peak in Mexico
1533-84 Ivan the Terrible rules Russia	**1534-42** Jacques Cartier voyages to Canada			**1500 onward:** Latin American gold and silver increase money supply in Europe, finance further exploration and settlement	**1438-1532** Inca civilization dominates Peru and nearby areas
1540 Jesuit Order founded: spearheads Counter Reformation	**1539-42** De Soto explores southeast U.S.				
1541 Calvin starts Reformation in Geneva	**1540-42** Coronado explores Southwest		**1564** French found Fort Caroline in Florida, threatening Spanish trade routes	**1540** Horses brought by Europeans change Indian hunting methods	**1577-1655** Spanish missionaries work with Indians in Southeast
1558-1603 Elizabeth I reigns in England	**1576** English begin search for Northwest Passage		**1565** Spaniards build a fort at St. Augustine and expel French		
1588 Spanish Armada defeated	**1598** Juan de Oñate settles New Mexico	**1559-70** League of the Iroquois formed in today's New York State			
1589-1610 Henry IV reigns in France					

1600

WORLD EVENTS	EXPLORATION and SETTLEMENT	POLITICS	MILITARY	ECONOMICS and SCIENCE	RELIGION, ARTS and PEOPLE
1603-25 James I reigns in England	**1607** Jamestown colony founded in Virginia	**c. 1607** Powhatan Confederacy formed in Virginia		**1609** Captain John Smith starts cultivation of Indian corn in Virginia	**1609** Anglican church established in Virginia
1618-48 Thirty Years' War ravages Europe	**1608** Champlain founds Quebec	**1619** America's first legislative body meets in Virginia		**1612** John Rolfe develops effective method of curing tobacco	**1620** Congregationalists reach New England
1625-49 Charles I reigns in England	**1609** Henry Hudson sails up Hudson River	**1620** Mayflower Compact	**1622** Indians massacre Jamestown settlers	**1619** First African Negroes sold in Virginia; first ironworks opened	**1630-51** William Bradford writes his history *Of Plymouth Plantation*
1633 William Laud becomes Archbishop of Canterbury	**1620** Pilgrims found Plymouth	**1622** Maine granted to Sir Ferdinando Gorges and Captain John Mason		**1629** Dutch set up patroon estates along Hudson	**1633** First English-speaking Roman Catholic group arrives, in Maryland
	1623 New Hampshire settled			**1636 onward:** Fishing industry expands in Massachusetts	**1636** Harvard College founded
	1624 Dutch settle Manhattan			**1639** First printing press in Massachusetts	**1639** Baptists organized as a church by Roger Williams, in Providence
	1630-43 Puritan "Great Migration" settles Massachusetts			**1640 onward:** Colonial crafts develop	**1640** *Bay Psalm Book* is first book printed in the colonies
1644-1912 Manchu Dynasty rules China	**1633** Maryland founded		**1643** New England Confederation established		**1641-1700** "Colonial" style of architecture evolves
1645 Puritans execute Archbishop Laud	**1635** First settlement in Connecticut		**1644** Second Indian massacre in Virginia		**1642-47** First system of public schools founded in Massachusetts
1649 Charles I executed; Cromwell establishes Commonwealth	**1636** Roger Williams settles Providence	**1647** Rhode Island's liberal constitution adopted			**1649** Maryland Act of Toleration passed
	1638 Swedes settle on Delaware River		**1655** Dutch occupy Swedish colony on Delaware	**1651-1767** Series of Navigation Acts regulate colonial trade	**1650** Anne Bradstreet writes *The Tenth Muse*, collection of poems
			1664 English take New Amsterdam	**1652-82** Pine Tree shilling minted	**1654** First group of Jews arrives, in New Amsterdam
		1665 Duke's Law established in New York	**1673-74** Dutch temporarily reoccupy New York		**1662** Michael Wigglesworth writes poem, "Day of Doom," a Calvinist version of the last judgment

France revokes Edict of Nantes **1688** England's "Glorious Revolution" ends absolutism **1688-97** War of League of Augsburg	explore Mississippi to Arkansas River **1682** LaSalle reaches mouth of Mississippi and claims Louisiana for France **1682** Penn founds Philadelphia	Government" becomes Pennsylvania's constitution **1691** Massachusetts Bay takes over Plymouth Colony and Maine **1696** Board of Trade assumes administration of colonies	place in Virginia **1689** Revolutions erupt in Virginia, Maryland and Massachusetts **1689-91** Leisler leads rebellion in New York **1689-97** King William's War	from Maine and Carolinas **1680 onward:** Middle and northern colonies export grain, animals, lumber, whale products, etc., to compensate for less profitable tobacco **1690 onward:** Madagascar rice grown successfully in South Carolina **1690 onward:** Importation of slaves greatly increases	poems **1683 onward:** Heavy immigration of Germans, Scotch-Irish and French **1690** Benjamin Harris publishes first newspaper, in Boston **1692** Salem witch trials held **1693** William and Mary College founded
1700					
1701-13 War of Spanish Succession **1714-27** George I, first Hanoverian king, reigns in England **1720** Tibet becomes a tributary of China **1727-60** George II reigns in England **1740-48** War of Austrian Succession makes Prussia a major power **1740-80** Maria Theresa of Austria reigns as "king" of Hungary **1740-86** Frederick the Great reigns in Prussia	**1701** Cadillac founds Detroit **1716-50** Appalachian Piedmont region settled **1718** French found New Orleans **1720** First settlement made in Vermont **1733** Georgia founded **1741** Vitus Bering discovers Alaskan mainland **1744-54** Pennsylvanians and Virginians move westward **1749** Halifax, Nova Scotia, founded **1749** Ohio Company starts surveys of Ohio Valley	**1701** Delaware gets separate government from Pennsylvania **1702** East and West Jersey united as royal province of New Jersey **1704** New York Assembly seizes tax power from royal governor **1712** North Carolina gets its own governor, separates from South Carolina **1715** 5th Lord Baltimore restored to proprietorship of Maryland	**1702-13** Queen Anne's War **1711-12** Indians lose Tuscarora War in North Carolina **1715-28** Yamassee Wars threaten settlers on Southeast borders **1718** Blackbeard the pirate killed by Virginia expedition **1739-42** War of Jenkins' Ear **1744-48** King George's War	**1700 onward:** Shipbuilding booms in New England **1700 onward:** Plantation system of Virginia, Maryland and Carolina reaches full development **1721** Inoculation for smallpox begins in Boston **1730 onward:** New England whaling industry flourishes **1730-40** Long rifle developed in Pennsylvania **1732** First stagecoach line, across New Jersey, begins **1732** Hat Act restricts colonial industry **1733** Molasses Act tries to restrict colonial trade to British Empire **1744 onward:** Indigo becomes a major southern crop **1748-59** Jared Eliot writes *Essays upon Field-Husbandry in New-England*	**1701** Yale College founded **1704** First organ built, in Philadelphia **1706** First Presbyterian group organized, in Philadelphia **1709-41** William Byrd writes his diaries and annals in Virginia **1716** First theater built, in Williamsburg **1717** Mother Goose rhymes and tunes published in Boston **1726-56** Jonathan Edwards and George Whitefield lead Great Awakening (religious revival) **1730** John Smibert stages first art exhibition, in Boston **1732-57** *Poor Richard Almanack* published **1734** Protestants emigrate from Salzburg to Georgia **1734-35** Zenger Case occurs **1746** College of New Jersey (Princeton) opens
1750					
1751 Clive defeats French in India **1755** Lisbon earthquake kills 30,000 **1756-63** Seven Years' War: England ends France's colonial aspirations **1759-88** Charles III reigns in Spain **1760-1820** George III reigns in England **1762-96** Catherine the Great reigns in Russia **1768-74** War between Russia and Turkey	**1764** St. Louis founded by French **1767-71** Boone visits Kentucky **1769-84** Fray Junípero Serra founds nine Franciscan missions in California **1772** John Sevier and James Robertson organize independent republic of Watauga within present Tennessee	**1754** Albany Convention meets **1758** Treaty of Easton signed between Pennsylvania and western Indians **1761** Writs of Assistance case tried in Boston **1763** British Proclamation forbids settlement west of Alleghenies **1764** Committee of Correspondence formed in Boston **1765** Stamp Act passed and protested **1766** Parliament repeals Stamp Act; asserts authority in Declaratory Act **1767** New York Assembly suspended for refusing to quarter troops **1768** Massachusetts denounces Townshend Acts; other colonies follow **1769** Virginia House of Burgesses protests Parliamentary Acts and is dissolved **1770** Boston Massacre **1773** Boston Tea Party **1774** Parliament passes Intolerable Acts **1774** First Continental Congress meets	**1754-63** French and Indian War **1755** Braddock is defeated in Pennsylvania **1760** Canada falls to British **1763** Pontiac leads Indian rebellion **1766** British destroy Liberty Pole in New York; Sons of Liberty clash with redcoats **1768** British troops arrive in Boston **1771** Regulators fight Battle of Alamance in North Carolina **1772** Customs schooner *Gaspee* burned in Rhode Island	**1750** Jacob Yoder develops flatboat in Philadelphia **1751** New England colonies forbidden to print paper money **1751** John Bartram publishes *Observations* on American plants **1752** Franklin experiments with lightning rod **1752** First general hospital opens in Philadelphia **1761** Harvard astronomical expedition goes to Newfoundland **1764** Business slumps in colonies **1765** First medical school opens, at College of Philadelphia **1765** New York, Philadelphia, Boston organize strict nonimportation agreements **1766** British modify trade laws **1767** Townshend Acts cause revival of nonimportation in colonies **1769** More stringent nonimportation agreements organized **1769-70** David Rittenhouse makes planetary observations **1770** Townshend Acts revised; colonial merchants work for conciliation **1773** East India Company granted tea monopoly **1773** First publicly supported mental hospital opens, in Williamsburg, Virginia	**1750 onward:** "Georgian" architecture develops **1751** Franklin's Academy, later University of Pennsylvania, opens **1754** King's College, now Columbia, opens **1756** Princeton's Nassau Hall, largest structure in colonies, is completed **1756-72** John Woolman writes his *Journal* **1759** Francis Hopkinson, later a signer of the Declaration, composes first secular song by a native American, "My Days Have Been So Wondrous Free" **1760-74** John Singleton Copley develops portrait style in Boston **1761** St. Cecilia Society, first musical group, founded, in Charleston, South Carolina **1766** Methodists organize a church in New York **1767** Thomas Godfrey's "The Prince of Parthia" is first native play to be professionally staged, in Philadelphia **1767** "Yankee Doodle" referred to in first American opera libretto **1768** John Dickinson writes *Letters from a Farmer in Pennsylvania*

FOR FURTHER READING

These books were selected for their interest and authority in the preparation of this volume, and for their usefulness to readers seeking additional information on specific points. An asterisk (*) marks works available in both hard-cover and paperback editions; a dagger (†) indicates availability only in paperback.

GENERAL READING

Andrews, Charles M., *The Colonial Period of American History* (4 vols.). Yale University Press, 1934-1938.

Carman, H. J., Syrett, H. C., and Wishy, B. W., *A History of the American People* (Vol. I). Alfred A. Knopf, 1960.

Hofstadter, R., Miller, W., and Aaron, D., *The American Republic* (Vol. I). Prentice-Hall, 1959.

Malone, Dumas, and Rauch, Basil, *Empire for Liberty* (Vol. I). Appleton-Century-Crofts, 1960.

Morison, Samuel Eliot, and Commager, Henry Steele, *The Growth of the American Republic* (Vol. I). Oxford University Press, 1962.

†Rossiter, Clinton L., *The First American Revolution*. Harcourt, Brace & World, 1956.

Wertenbaker, Thomas J., *Founding of American Civilization: The Middle Colonies*. Scribner's, 1938.

*Wright, Louis B., *The Cultural Life of the American Colonies: 1607-1763*. Harper & Row, 1957.

DISCOVERY AND EXPLORATION (CHAPTERS 1 AND 2)

*Bakeless, John E., *The Eyes of Discovery*. Peter Smith, 1962.

Bishop, Morris, *Champlain: The Life of Fortitude*. Alfred A. Knopf, 1948.

Bolton, Herbert E., *The Spanish Borderlands*. Yale University Press, 1921.

*Bourne, Edward G., *Spain in America, 1450-1580*. Barnes & Noble, 1962.

*Brebner, John B., *The Explorers of North America, 1492-1806*. Macmillan, 1933.

*De Voto, Bernard, *The Course of Empire*. Houghton Mifflin, 1952.

Dockstader, Frederick J., *Indian Art in America*. New York Graphic Society, 1961.

La Farge, Oliver, *A Pictorial History of the American Indian*. Crown Publishers, Inc., 1956.

Lamb, Harold, *New Found World*. Doubleday, 1955.

Martin, P. S., Quimby, G. I., and Collier, D., *Indians before Columbus*. University of Chicago Press, 1947.

*Morison, Samuel Eliot, *Admiral of the Ocean Sea: A Life of Christopher Columbus*. Little, Brown, 1942.

Nute, Grace Lee, *Caesars of the Wilderness*. Appleton-Century-Crofts, 1943.

*Penrose, Boies, *Travel and Discovery in the Renaissance, 1420-1620*. Harvard University Press, 1955.

*Quinn, David B., *Raleigh and the British Empire*. Macmillan, 1949.

Rowse, A. L., *The Elizabethans and America*. Harper & Row, 1959.

Underhill, Ruth, *Red Man's America*. University of Chicago Press, 1953.

Wissler, Clark, *Indians of the United States*. Doubleday, 1940.

*Wormington, H. M., *Ancient Man in North America*. Denver Museum of Natural History, 1957.

Wrong, George M., *The Rise and Fall of New France* (2 vols.). Macmillan, 1928.

THE ENGLISH COLONIES (CHAPTERS 3 AND 4)

Bailyn, Bernard, *The New England Merchants in the Seventeenth Century*. Harvard University Press, 1955.

Channing, Edward, *A History of the United States* (Vols. I & II). Macmillan, 1927-1928.

Chitwood, Oliver Perry, *A History of Colonial America*. Harper & Row, 1961.

Craven, Wesley F., *The Southern Colonies in the Seventeenth Century, 1607-1689*. Louisiana State University Press, 1949.

Ettinger, Amos A., *James Edward Oglethorpe, Imperial Idealist*. Oxford University Press, 1936.

*Miller, Perry, *Roger Williams: His Contribution to the American Tradition*. Bobbs-Merrill, 1953.

Morison, Samuel Eliot, *Builders of the Bay Colony*. Houghton Mifflin, 1930.

*Notestein, Wallace, *The English People on the Eve of Colonization: 1603-1630*. Harper & Row, 1954.

Osgood, H. L., *The American Colonies in the Eighteenth Century* (4 vols.). Peter Smith, 1958. *The American Colonies in the Seventeenth Century* (3 vols.). Peter Smith, 1957.

*Parrington, Vernon L., *Main Currents in American Thought*. Harcourt, Brace & World, 1939.

Pound, Arthur, *The Penns of Pennsylvania and England*. Macmillan, 1932.

Rugg, W. K., *Unafraid: A Life of Anne Hutchinson*. Houghton Mifflin, 1930.

Wertenbaker, Thomas J., *The Shaping of Colonial Virginia*. Russell & Russell, 1958. *Torchbearer of the Revolution: The Story of Bacon's Rebellion and Its Leader*. Princeton University Press, 1940.

Willison, George F., *Saints and Strangers*. Reynal & Company, 1945.

Wright, Louis B., *The Atlantic Frontier*. Cornell University Press, 1959.

A BUSY LAND (CHAPTER 5)

*Bridenbaugh, Carl, *The Colonial Craftsman*. New York University Press, 1950.

Clark, V. S., *History of Manufactures in the United States, 1607-1928* (Vol. I). Peter Smith, 1949.

Franklin, John Hope, *From Slavery to Freedom: A History of American Negroes*. Alfred A. Knopf, 1956.

Gray, L. C., *The History of Agriculture in the Southern United States to 1860* (Vol. I). Peter Smith, 1949.

Greene, E. B., and Harrington, V. D., *American Population before the Federal Census of 1790*. Columbia University Press, 1932.

Harper, Lawrence A., *English Navigation Laws: A Seventeenth-Century Experiment in Social Engineering*. Columbia University Press, 1939.

Morris, Richard B., *Government and Labor in Early America*. Columbia University Press, 1946.

Nettels, Curtis P., *The Roots of American Civilization*. Appleton-Century-Crofts, 1938.

Stampp, Kenneth M., *The Peculiar Institution*. Alfred A. Knopf, 1956.

U.S. Bureau of the Census, *Historical Statistics of the United States, Colonial Times to 1957*. 1960.

Wertenbaker, Thomas J., *The First Americans, 1607-1690*. Macmillan, 1927.

CREATING A NEW CIVILIZATION (CHAPTER 6)

Boorstin, Daniel J., *The Americans: The Colonial Experience*. Random House, 1958.

Bridenbaugh, Carl, *Cities in Revolt*. Alfred A. Knopf, 1955. *Cities in the Wilderness*. Alfred A. Knopf, 1955.

Flexner, James T., *American Painting: First Flowers of Our Wilderness*. Houghton Mifflin, 1947.

Hindle, Brooke, *The Pursuit of Science in Revolutionary America, 1735-1789*. University of North Carolina Press, 1956.

*Miller, Perry, *Jonathan Edwards*. William Sloane, 1949. *The New England Mind: From Colony to Province*. Harvard University Press, 1953. *Orthodoxy in Massachusetts, 1630-1650*. Peter Smith, 1959.

*Morison, Samuel Eliot, *The Intellectual Life of Colonial New England*. New York University Press, 1956.

Morrison, Hugh, *Early American Architecture: From the First Colonial Settlements to the National Period*. Oxford University Press, 1952.

*Starkey, Marion, *The Devil in Massachusetts*. Peter Smith, 1962.

Trinterud, L. J., *The Forming of an American Tradition*. Westminster Press, 1949.

*Tyler, Moses Coit, *A History of American Literature: 1607-1765*. Cornell University Press, 1949.

*Wertenbaker, Thomas J., *The Golden Age of Colonial Culture*. New York University Press, 1949.

Wish, Harvey, *Society and Thought in America* (Vol. I). David McKay, 1950.

THE COMING OF THE REVOLUTION (CHAPTER 7)

Dickerson, O. M., *The Navigation Acts and the American Revolution*. University of Pennsylvania Press, 1951.

Gipson, Lawrence H., *The British Empire before the American Revolution* (10 vols.). Alfred A. Knopf, 1956-1961. *The Coming of the Revolution: 1763-1775*. Harper & Row, 1954.

*Knollenberg, Bernhard, *Origin of the American Revolution: 1759-1766*. Macmillan, 1960.

Miller, John C., *Origins of the American Revolution*. Stanford University Press, 1959.

Morgan, Edmund S. and Helen M., *The Stamp Act Crisis*. University of North Carolina Press, 1953.

†Morris, Richard B., *The American Revolution: A Short History*. Van Nostrand, 1955.

*Namier, Sir Lewis, *England in the Age of the American Revolution*. St. Martin's Press, 1961.

Plumb, J. H., *The First Four Georges*. Macmillan, 1957.

Schlesinger, Arthur M., *The Colonial Merchants and the American Revolution, 1763-1776*. Frederick Ungar, 1957.

ACKNOWLEDGMENTS

The editors of this book are particularly indebted to the following persons and institutions: Dr. Frederick J. Dockstader, Director, Museum of the American Indian, New York, New York; Dr. Loren C. Eiseley, University Professor of Anthropology and the History of Science, University of Pennsylvania; James W. Foster and Eugenia Holland, Maryland Historical Society; Helen C. McCormack, Gibbes Art Gallery, Charleston, South Carolina; David M. Reese, Telfair Academy of Arts and Sciences, Inc., Savannah, Georgia; Elizabeth Roth, New York Public Library Print Collection; and Marguerite H. Munson and Judy Higgins.

PICTURE CREDITS

INDEX

This symbol in front of a page number indicates a photograph or painting of the subject mentioned.